Terrorism, security and nationality

Acts of terrorism and political violence are on the increase throughout the world; nationalism in its ugliest forms threatens peace and security in many regions; the foundations of the modern state are continually under threat.

Terrorism, Security and Nationality shows how the concepts and techniques of political philosophy can be applied to the problems of terrorism, state violence and national identity. In doing so, it clarifies a wide range of issues in applied political philosophy, including the ethics of war, theories of state and nation, the relationship between communities and nationalisms, and the uneasy balance of human rights and national security.

Paul Gilbert examines the reasons for political violence and assesses the justifications put forward by its perpetrators: ethnicity, nationality and the interests of the state. He analyses their conflicting notions of what constitutes a political community and provides a much needed philosophical critique of contrasting accounts of national identity.

A comprehensive philosophical study of political violence, *Terrorism, Security and Nationality* will be essential reading for students of politics and philosophy as well as all those seeking to understand one of the most intractable problems of our time.

Paul Gilbert is Senior Lecturer in Philosophy at the University of Hull. He is the author of *Human Relationships: A Philosophical Introduction* (1991).

Terrorism, security and nationality

An introductory study in applied political philosophy

Paul Gilbert

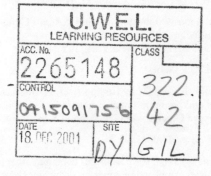

London and New York

First published 1994
by Routledge
11 New Fetter Lane, London EC4P 4EE

Simultaneously published in the USA and Canada
by Routledge
29 West 35th Street, New York, NY 10001

Typeset in Baskerville by Computerset, Harmondsworth
Printed and bound in Great Britain by
Mackays of Chatham PLC, Chatham, Kent.

Printed on acid free paper

British Library Cataloguing in Publication Data
A catalogue record for this book is available from the British Library.

Library of Congress Cataloging in Publication Data
Gilbert, Paul –
    Terrorism, security, and nationality: an introductory study in applied
    political philosophy/Paul Gilbert.
    p.cm.
    Includes bibliographical references and index.
    1. Terrorism. 2. Nationalism. 3. National security.
    4. Political science–Philosophy. I. Title.
    HV6431.G54 1994   93–48161
    363.3′2–dc20   CIP

ISBN 0–415–09175–6 (hbk)   0–415–09176–4 (pbk)

Contents

Preface and acknowledgements

Writing this book over the last couple of years has been a dispiriting experience. As it goes to press, policies which successfully address the reasons for terrorism close to home have not yet been found. Abroad, hopes for a dramatic reduction in state terror following the spread of democratic institutions seem to have been misplaced. Instead the horrors of internal and irregular war have immeasurably increased. Nationalism in its ugliest forms menaces communal peace across the world, and what used to look like a limited problem occasioning sporadic local violence now again threatens the foundations of the modern state.

The book began in a symposium organised by the Society of Applied Philosophy at the 1988 World Congress of Philosophy and at the Society's Annual Conference the following year. My thanks to the Society and in particular to Brenda Almond for the opportunity these offered. Earlier versions of some parts were presented at the 1990 and 1991 workshops of the European Consortium for Political Research under the chairmanship of Alex Schmid and Michael Freeman, and at the 1990 International Society for Study of European Ideas conference under that of Eugene Kamenka: my thanks to them also. Details of previously published versions of some of the material in the book are given in the References.

The colleagues and students at Hull and elsewhere to whom I am indebted for their comments and suggestions are too numerous to mention. But I should like to pay particular thanks to David George, Martin Hughes, Kathleen Lennon, Bhikhu Parech and Gerry Wallace.

Finally my thanks are due to Margaret Snowden for her indispensable assistance in preparing the manuscript for publication.

Chapter 1

Introduction

Political philosophy traditionally concerns itself with the question of what a political community *should* be like: how justice is to be achieved within it, what degree of equality is compatible with a desirable degree of freedom and so forth. Political philosophy concerns itself for the most part, then, with ethical issues which underlie the political contests between parties contending for power within established states. Yet beneath the ethical questions lurks a metaphysical one: what *is* a political community?[1]

The question of what constitutes a political community is seldom at issue in the politics of established states. Political parties tend to agree on what community it is that they seek to represent and they differ only on what it should be like. But this question is very commonly at issue in nationalist conflicts, where what are to count as the communities to be represented takes precedence over the question of what they should eventually be like. And underlying the political disagreement is commonly a metaphysical one concerning the criteria for identifying distinct political communities.

It is with the metaphysical question that this book is ultimately concerned, though its approach may seem oblique and inconclusive. No doubt a more direct method would be possible. It might, however, be a less illuminating one if our purpose in posing the metaphysical question is to seek an understanding of constitutional conflict, of nationalist causes and of the violence to which they frequently give rise. For this we need an account not purely theoretical, but applicable to the practical problems of creating and sustaining political communities.

The approach adopted here exemplifies in two respects applied political philosophy. First, its interest is in grasping how political conflicts can spring from philosophical disagreements. It is, therefore, concerned with identifying and assessing the conceptual assumptions involved, with a view to developing a reflective and critical attitude to these conflicts and their resolution. Second, it draws the philosophical concepts it investigates from the political behaviour to which they are applied, since it would be surprising if this behaviour could be explained in terms of notions that had no place in the thinking of its agents.

Our aim is to seek to understand behaviour that is often, on the face of it, shockingly irrational by reconstructing a pattern of reasoning behind it. In some cases this will draw upon notions *acknowledged* by its agents to play a part in their deliberations. In other cases it will not: revealing the assumptions we ourselves unreflectively make can often be as illuminating to us, in understanding our own behaviour, as revealing the assumptions of others can be in illuminating theirs. The aim, however, is not only to understand but to criticise – to assess the plausibility of the patterns of reasoning exemplified in political behaviour and to suggest alternatives.

The extent to which understanding and criticism are *possible* raises a large philosophical question concerning the commensurability of divergent assumptions about the nature of political communities and about the limits of political action. Again my approach will be to abjure a direct answer. Instead I attempt to locate apparently irreconcilable differences in the contrasting roles of political agents contending for power. It is to these contrasts that the Janus-faced character of political action in areas of conflict within the state is referable. What appears to its agents as an heroic stand strikes others as a futile gesture, what is justified by government as the maintenance of law and order is attacked as political repression and so on. Political actions have no single significance; for what people do is determined not only by what they intend but by what behaviour of that kind is understood by others to be, whatever its agents' intentions. It is those in positions of power who preeminently control the conventions in terms of which political behaviour is understood. Even to succeed in *acting* in a way that carries a contrary message can be a triumph.

The book begins by discussing a form of political behaviour which epitomises this unsettling phenomenon – terrorism. Is it, as those who undertake it intend, war? Or is it, as the state treats it, merely crime? An understanding of its equivocal nature shows, I shall suggest, why terrorism is so often the resort of nationalists and others who differ with the established state as to the political community to be represented. Terrorism exemplifies, too, a larger uncertainty: is it a legitimate tactic to be employed in the defence of a political community, or is it a mode of behaviour that any community must suppress as threatening to destroy, not just a particular community, but the social relations essential to *any* political community?

A similar question can be posed concerning the security operations of the state: do they serve to protect communal relations, or do they undermine them in pursuit of sectional interests? Are they legitimate acts of law enforcement, or can they themselves constitute state terrorism? Indeed, is the state, through its provision of security, the foundation of community, or an instrument of its oppression?

There is, I believe, no detached point of view from which we can expect definitive answers to these questions. What is clear is that we all do fear unpredictable violence, whether from the state or its opponents, as a threat to the order upon which our communal life depends. Any political organisation aims to maintain social order. But what kinds of group might reasonably expect to have their own ordered and harmonious social life?

This question brings us to the problem of national identity. In a world of nation states the paradigmatic political community is a national one. What, though, constitutes a nation? My answer ties the criteria for nationhood to the requirements of statehood, and finds the traditional accounts presupposed in many nationalist campaigns deficient. Political communities, I conclude, are ethical communities, whose criteria of identity lie in their capacity to provide for a good communal life. Whether the nation, as represented by the modern state, can perform this ethical function must remain an open question.

Chapter 2

Terrorism and unjust war

MINDLESS VIOLENCE

Bombings which cause death and injury to civilian citizens, as in the IRA campaign, may be taken as paradigmatic of contemporary terrorist attacks – attacks arousing outrage and anger in equal measure to the fear and uneasiness they induce. A 'public' reaction, drawn from eyewitnesses, police or politicians gives voice to the former rather than the latter. But a public reaction, one reported or broadcast, is selective and formulaic. Incomprehension, to which it frequently resorts, can itself, in place of explanation, be a kind of security. There are many formulae for shutting off the worrisome search for understanding such violence: it can be seen as 'mindless', 'psychopathic' or 'animal' behaviour, for example. Clearly these descriptions require some investigation even if they can do nothing to account for the mood of outrage they are intended to express, since they evidently do nothing to justify it. Mindlessness or mental illness seem rather occasions for pity, while dumb animals of a ferocious temper are shown a respect not accorded to the terrorist.

Is there something wrong with the mind of the terrorist? Or has he put in abeyance human compunctions against a mode of conduct that our deeper drives incline us to? Neither story has any general plausibility.

'Mindless violence', on one understanding of the phrase, is that for which no further reason can be offered – which seems, at least, to be engaged in for its own sake, or maybe because it is enjoyed. The ranks of terrorists may include those who are acting this way without espousing any cause; perhaps the cause that they espouse provides only an occasion for or a rationalisation of violence. Yet there is no reason to think that terrorism in itself is of this kind. Its violent acts

are mostly done for further reasons and, we should not doubt, often
with a heavy heart. The mindlessly violent may be more of a liability than an asset in such a cause.

By the same token the psychopath, while no stranger to terrorist
causes, does not exemplify terrorism's essential character. Acting for
reasons which appear in no way to justify the extent and degree of
his violence, he sees, at the time, no disproportion and, in consequence, no need for exculpation. The terrorist, on the contrary, seeks
to persuade us of the reasonableness of his acts, fantastical as they
may sometimes seem. He appeals on the whole to principles in ordinary currency, while even the fanatic appeals to principles that are
shared at least by true believers; he does not make *himself* the
measure of the rightness of his acts, however opaque it may be to
those beyond his circle.

There is nothing obviously wrong with the *mind* of the terrorist.
Indeed for the most part he does what most of us would do – rightly or wrongly – if called upon to do it. The days are gone when it was
thought to be a special calling, or that it required a special stamp of
character, to engage in killing one's fellow men and women; now
everyone, or at least, for here lurks a remnant of old belief, all males,
may be conscripted to perpetrate acts that result with certainty in
death or dreadful suffering. It cannot be a capacity for such acts that
sets the terrorist mind apart from others. Nor is it a greater preparedness to perform them. The terrorist characteristically occupies
a place within a structure of command analogous to that of a recognised military force. He obeys his orders but takes them from a
different source from the serviceman: neither is notable for declining
to obey orders that strike him as morally repugnant. There is no evidence that the terrorist shows less repugnance or greater
preparedness to obey them. Indeed, perhaps the contrary is true, for
terrorist groups frequently fragment over their choice of tactics,
including over which are and which are not acceptable from a moral
point of view.

There is at least a formal difference between the view that the terrorist mind is abnormal in fostering acts of cruelty or callousness
which others similarly situated would not be disposed to commit,
and the view that he acts from instincts common to all, but which
most people hold in check, recognising and fearing their brutish origins and outcomes or acknowledging the reasons for restraint. Many
of the arguments against the former view of terrorism go over to the

latter. It is worth pausing briefly however to consider the picture of terrorism as instinctual violence unrestrained.

We cannot here adequately address the large question of whether *man* in the ungendered or, indeed, the gendered sense, is by nature violent – prone to attacks upon his fellow men generally or, more specifically, upon those who do not form part of some social group within which he is peaceable.[1] It is worth noting, though, that whatever account is offered there is no prospect of providing a good *evolutionary* argument for it. The identification and explanation of human traits, such as some putative forms of aggressiveness, on the grounds that they conduce to the survival of the species are notoriously perilous. All we know from evolutionary theory is that whatever genetically determined traits we have are not disastrously maladaptive – or have not been up to now. But in that case it is hard to see what might justify us in collecting together a multifarious collection of phenomena – muggings, gang fights, inter-state wars and terrorism, for example – as manifestations of a *single* trait at all.

One possibility would be to see, behind the apparent variety, some relatively fixed and inflexible pattern of behaviour of the kind which evolutionary theory is well adapted to explain. To do that one would need to identify it as, in at least very many circumstances, *irrational*, mindless in the sense not of lacking reason, but of being contrary to it – a routine fallen into rather than a means adopted as best fitted to its objective. This was, it seems, Freud's view, when he wrote[2] that men's 'neighbour is . . . someone who tempts them to satisfy their aggressiveness on him, to exploit his capacity for work without compensation, to use him sexually without his consent, to seize his possessions . . . to humiliate him, to cause him pain, to torture and to kill him. Homo homini lupus' – man is a wolf to man.

Yet it is hard to believe that the terrorist's tactics are not predominantly judged to be best fitted to his ends, however cruel, or even because so cruel, in execution. Their remorseless repetitiveness is not that of a routine unadapted to particular circumstances, but precisely that of a means adapted as best expressing the terrorist's implacable determination to achieve his ends. There are no grounds here for detecting the eruption of the beast in man.

To be sure, this notion is more properly a theological than a scientific one. The beast provides a supernatural rather than a naturalistic explanation of the violence attributed to it. And it explains that violence as morally repugnant. Only thus could it figure as characterising the culprit responsible for terrorist outrages. How might it do so?

UNJUST WAR

Terrorism, it has been suggested,[3] 'essentially means any method of war which consists in intentionally attacking those who ought not to be attacked'. This is intended as a definition of terrorism. What motivates it is the desire to capture what it is that excites the outrage which we commonly feel about terrorism. The suggestion would be that terrorism transgresses a prohibition on attacking other people unless they fall into some special category of person unprotected from attack. We take it for granted that attacking them is morally wrong, because it is both wicked and unjust. It is wicked because it is pitiless – it fails to betray a recognition of others as fellow human beings whose lives demand a certain kind of respect. It is unjust because it singles out some as victims without good reason, simply because it suits their assailants to do so.

What we take for granted here is something deeply rooted at least in European culture, and no doubt well beyond it. Its roots are partly classical, partly Christian, presupposing a common humanity in virtue of which a certain attitude to people is appropriate, an attitude forfeited only by those who directly or indirectly fail to demonstrate it themselves. Such a presupposition is what underlies the medieval theory of the just war, and it is this theory that motivates many contemporary accounts of terrorism which represent it as something necessarily abhorrent.

I shall term this model of terrorism the unjust war model. It typically assumes – what will later need to be examined – that terrorism is a form of warfare. Or, rather more cautiously, it assumes that it is sufficiently similar to war to be judged in accordance with the rules of war. For it assumes that there is a certain category of violent conflict whose entitlement to be termed 'war' stems from the fact that it is normally waged in accordance with certain rules.[4] The analogy with games may be helpful here. The rules of football support judgements as to what should and should not be done by the participants. In rough games many rules may be broken, but if too many are broken the game ceases to be recognisable as football at all. Just war theory can be viewed as sketching out what war is by detailing the rules for its proper pursuit. And the unjust war model of terrorism is one which indicates some kind of departure from the rules as that which makes the activity terrorism, whether it is still sufficiently within the rules to count as war or not.

A just war theory seeks to identify a class of permissible exceptions to the injunction, 'thou shalt not kill'. It does so in two stages. First it identifies a set of circumstances in which people may justifiably band together to offer violence to others, that is to say, to wage a war against them. This provides the *jus ad bellum*, the right to go to war, which preeminently involves having a just cause. Second, it identifies what kind of violence is permissible in these circumstances, the *jus in bello* or what is right in war, which involves not using wrongful means in pursuit of one's cause. Since there is no single just war theory[5] but rather a tradition of thinking about the justification of war, no comprehensive and fully coherent account of when it is right to go to war or what it is right to do in war should be expected of it. It is true that just war theory is generally presented as a single theory, and different theorists attempt to make it coherent and plausible in different ways, reflecting in part their different moral reactions as to what is and what is not permissible in war. This is not our present task. Rather we are looking to the tradition for explanations of some of our moral reactions. Since these are commonly confused and fail to find clear grounds for the distinctions they evince it is unlikely that the body of theory on which they draw is lucid, unitary and consistent. We should not then expect just war theory to yield a clear and uncontroversial answer to the question, who ought not to be intentionally attacked, so that putatively *terrorist* acts can be identified as those which are excluded.

There are, broadly speaking, two potentially divergent strands in just war theory. Indeed the theory may be regarded as an uneasy conflation of two quite disparate models. The older of the two sees *jus ad bellum* as consisting in the *punishment* of a wrong that has been committed, for example through some unjustified attack. *Jus in bello* accordingly consists in counter-attacking only to the extent required to punish the wrong-doer and, as far as possible, to remedy this wrong, avoiding any attacks upon those innocent of it. We may dub this punitive just war theory. The other strand, which predominates in the influence of just war theory in modern international law views *jus ad bellum* as consisting principally in the *prevention* of a wrong by means of self-defensive operations. *Jus in bello* consists, therefore, in doing no more than is required for repulsing an attacker or recovering territory, thus not attacking those not involved in the threat against one. Let us call this defensive just war theory.

While these two forms may be assimilated into a single just war theory, they do more than merely emphasise the distinction between retribution for a wrong and the prevention of it. The punitive theory justifies attacks in war by drawing on an analogy with legal punishment, in which an individual may be made to suffer, arguably even killed, for wrongs that he has committed against the community. But it is the civil authorities that administer punishment, not the individual who is wronged. Analogously the punitive theory lays stress on the need for *proper authority* in the waging of war, for only such an authority can distinguish public wrong from private injury, and in consequence act from the *right intention* of bringing about a better state of affairs, rather than reacting out of individual anger and animosity in a way that prejudices the chances of long-term peace and justice.

By contrast the defensive theory construes just war on the analogy of individuals' rights to defend themselves when they are threatened. Someone who does so is not so much acting for the best as acting naturally, having a right, because not a blameable, intention. When a group does likewise in a defensive war it acts as a group, rather than as a gang of individuals, only if it acts under proper authority – one, that is, which can judge whether the group is being threatened with a wrong and can react on its behalf.

Both forms of the just war theory stress the moral wrongness to which justified war is a response. But they locate it quite differently. For the punitive theory the wrong that is done must be identifiable otherwise than as a breach of the rules of war. Attacking someone is recognisable, other things being equal, as wrong, and the rules of war permit, indeed require, it to be punished. One side in the ensuing conflict is therefore the wrong-doer and the other may do whatever, but only whatever, will punish the aggressor.

The defensive theory by contrast perceives that in war, and in many situations leading to war, each side principally aims to defend itself. This they are permitted to do. What is morally wrong is to act in a way that goes beyond the requirements of self-defence. Wrong-doing is therefore identified in terms of breaches of the rules of war and having a just cause in terms of being a victim of such breaches. On the defensive theory, what is stressed is blame for infringements which may attach to both sides, while only one side could be acting justly in punishing an initial wrong as in the punitive theory.

The two forms of theory differ too in respect of their attitude to the efficacy of war as a means to its intended end. In both, war should be a last resort, but because the proper ends of war are different in the two theories, this is the case for different reasons. On the punitive theory it is because the evil of war is so great that all other means must be employed to persuade an aggressor to make reparation for the wrong he has perpetrated before war is resorted to. If this is not done, then it must be doubtful if the intention of waging war is simply the remedying of the wrong. On the defensive theory, war is a last resort because of the very nature of the threat to which it is a response. The existence of the threat indicates that for the defenders all other options have run out.

Correspondingly the *hope of success* required for a justified resort to arms in just war theory has a different force in its two versions. In the punitive theory war can be resorted to only if it is likely to succeed in remedying a wrong committed; for if it is unsuccessful no punishment will have been meted out and the last state would be morally worse than the first. On the defensive theory however there need be no considerable prospect of success for resistance to be justified, since there is no other way for the objective of security to be attained. One might, of course, take the view that resistance would be costly but futile. Yet to take this view is to place another end above that of the defence of the community.

It is evident from the outset that the two forms of the theory may well offer different answers to the question of who ought not to be attacked, even if commonly they will coincide. A counter-attack against an aggressor will commonly constitute self-defence and vice versa. But equally punitive counter-measures, while proportionate to the wrong done, may go beyond what is needed to secure one's territory, for what is needed for that may be a pre-emptive strike before any wrong is done. Those who may justifiably be attacked will differ in the two cases.

Similarly those involved in a threat to one's territorial security will commonly be implicated in the aggressor's guilt. But, as we shall see later, the guilty need pose no actual threat while those that do may not be guilty. Again different targets will be permissible, depending on which version of just war theory is appealed to. In each the *jus in bello* fits together with the *jus ad bellum*, the latter determining the former. It is, though, to the terrorist's alleged lack of *jus in bello* that we turn first.

TARGETING THE INNOCENT

When terrorism is thought of as 'any method of war which consists in intentionally attacking those who ought not to be attacked' it is the lack of *jus in bello* that is being picked out as its defining characteristic. This is implied by thinking of terrorism as a *method* of conducting a war, in the sense of a choice of tactics in war. Those who are attacked by terrorists are wrongly attacked, not because there is no justification for viewing them as an enemy against whom war is to be waged, but rather because there is no justification for attacking such people in *any* war. This view of terrorism is, in some form or other, the commonest kind of application of the unjust war model. It holds that the terrorist violates the principle of discrimination required for *jus in bello* under the theory of the just war: we may therefore call it the indiscriminate-violence view of terrorism.

The usual way to express the principle that terrorists are held to violate is to say that it is unjust to intentionally attack the *innocent*. Indeed terrorist acts, like the massacre at Enniskillen, are anathematised precisely as avoidably harming innocent people. This notion of innocence, understood as contrasted with guilt, is anchored, of course, in punitive just war theory, and its retention bespeaks the continued hold of these medieval ideas over us. But it is used, too, misleadingly, in defensive versions of the theory, where it connotes not lack of guilt but harmlessness. Already, then, the principle has two forms in relation to each of which the indiscriminate-violence view of terrorism needs examining. The notion of innocence as understood in the punitive theory is difficult to apply in a way that plausibly explains our common intuitions as to who may and who ought not to be attacked in war. Suppose legitimate military targets are 'the non-innocent' – those people 'engaged in an objectively unjust proceeding which the attacker has the right to make his concern'.[6] Then the properly authorised soldiers of the side with the just cause are not, so long as their methods do not contravene the rules of just conduct in war, legitimate targets. But surely *any* hostile soldier is a legitimate target or, at least, taking him to be so is a quite different matter from taking an ordinary citizen to be a legitimate target.

The model underlying punitive theory here is of course the immunity of officers of the law to attack by a criminal on grounds of self-defence. Yet it is one thing for a criminal to attack plain-clothes policemen thinking they are thugs intent on settling old scores with him, and quite another to attack some bystanders who offer no threat. In the former case he *believes* that his assailants are 'engaged in an objectively unjust proceeding' which he cannot believe of the bystanders. Then so it will be for all who fight in good faith, thinking their cause is just. The enemy soldiers are legitimate targets because they are believed to be non-innocent.

A greater difficulty concerns what it is to be *engaged* in an objectively unjust proceeding in such a way as to be a legitimate target.[7] One way to take this is to categorise as non-innocent whatever activity contributes to the unjust proceeding in such a way that the activity would not have occurred if that proceeding had not. In that case arms-factory workers as well as soldiers may be legitimate targets, but not 'harmless agricultural folk'.[8] Why though are the former *guilty* and the latter not? The reason must be that an intention to contribute to a proceeding in fact unjust is presumed to lie behind the activity. And if it is replied that the *intention* was merely to earn some money then at least a culpable lack of concern for the consequences must be present.

All this may seem to restrict the range of those who may be legitimately targeted to those knowingly and avoidably engaged in war. Yet this is to ignore two features of the punitive theory's emphasis on injustice as providing a cause of war, and thereby determining who should be targeted. Commonly this injustice will be in the form of military aggression which needs to be repelled. But aggression is only one way in which a state may seek to dominate people over whom it has no lawful authority. It may for example settle those people's lands with or without a war of aggression. In such circumstances it is evident that many not engaged in war itself may be regarded as legitimate targets because they are engaged in activity that furthers an injustice. Legitimate targets are perpetrators of injustice, so long as thus targeting them is proportionate to their offence.

It needs to be noted that this falls far short of the imputation of collective responsibility to the citizens of a state that acts unjustly. This as we shall see implies a conception of the relation between citizens and the state alien to just war theory. It is one thing for citizens to be held responsible for the state's proceedings *whatever* they are doing, and quite another to hold them responsible in virtue of particular activities which further the state's ambitions. This brings us to a second feature of punitive just war theory's emphasis on injustice relevant to the principle of discrimination. The *principal* targets of war are those who plan and organise the injustice, rather than those who pose a direct military threat. The latter may for example be far less guilty mercenaries who have to be targeted with regret only because those that command and control them are inaccessible.

It is these two features of the punitive theory that bear most closely on the terrorist's choice of apparently innocent people as targets. It needs to be said, though, that the view that terrorism comprises *only* attacks on those who ought not be attacked under the theory appears to be mistaken. Terrorism as generally understood is taken to include attacks on the state's security forces as well as on civilians. It cannot plausibly be claimed that these forces are not really engaged in military operations because they are involved in law enforcement, and so are not legitimate targets. If terrorism *is* to be treated as a method of war, in accordance with the unjust war model, then there must be *some* legitimate targets which the terrorists could attack in consistence with the rules of war. It is hard to see what else could constitute a legitimate target if not the security forces.

Terrorists commonly do justify their choice of targets. While public outrage at them may be explained by the application of just war notions, it is equally such notions that are commonly appealed to in their justification. If we consider some of the civilian targets intentionally selected by the IRA, defences drawn from punitive just war theory are available, though not necessarily adequate. For example builders employed on work in security-force bases can be represented as directly contributing to the enemy's war effort, and therefore as legitimate targets because they knowingly and avoidably engaged in this. Attacking them to some degree frustrates that war effort. Similarly, though not contributing to any war, judges are engaged in the administration of what is viewed as British occupation. By contrast, attacks on politicians are attacks on the planners and organisers of occupation: where accessible they can be targeted directly, not necessarily because this may help to end the occupation, but simply as retribution for it. In such cases we see especially clearly the application of punitive just war theory.

NON-COMBATANT IMMUNITY

The defensive theory has a different emphasis. This is partly because it is a more restricted theory; for while self-defence may provide a just cause under the punitive theory, this is not on account of the dangers but of the wrongfulness of the attack. In theory, then, some self-defensive acts, namely those mounted against an enemy with a just cause, will be unjust. The defensive theory concentrates instead on the justification provided by the fact that one is forestalling harm which an aggressor may intend, or one is restoring one's security against it. The defensive theory seeks to apply the principle of discrimination in a way that is independent of the justice of one's cause, so that the class of innocent (i.e. *harmless*) people can be identified as immune from legitimate attack whatever its source.[9]

Under the defensive theory the principal targets of war are *combatants*, for it is principally combatants who constitute a threat to one's security. What makes it legitimate to attack combatants but not, mostly, to attack civilians is that the former are *obstacles* to one's military goals, while the latter are not. This enables one to view the attack as aimed at removing the obstacle which necessitates incapacitating the man: it is not, as on the punitive theory, aimed directly at having some specific harmful effect on him as a person.[10] The soldier who is justifiably killed in battle can thus reflect either, 'they did not intend to harm me personally, so I cannot complain that I did not deserve it; I died simply because I happened to be a soldier' or, more heroically, 'they intended to harm me because I was a soldier; but I cannot complain because I undertook this role knowing its dangers'.[11] Which of these is appropriate depends on what we take the justification of killing in self-defence to consist in. The former reflection views it as an instance of the principle of double effect – that is to say as an effect that is foreseen but not intended in an act whose aim is simply that of security. The latter views it as an instance of the principle that other people are not to be used only as a means to one's ends, so that it is not because the other's death saves a life that he is killed (as when the cabin boy is killed and eaten by the survivors of a shipwreck) but because his own ends include accepting the possibility of such a death (as when the dying captain asks to be killed in order to conserve the lifeboat's water). Which of these conceptions should we follow?

One difficulty with the first example is that it makes it hard to see how far non-combatant immunity should properly be extended. If one can argue that it is the combatant who is targeted and not the man, can one not argue equally that it is the farmer who is targeted (because he feeds combatants) and not the man? If it is replied that being a combatant is a role that can be enacted only in war, while the farmer farms through peace as well as war, then let it be as a supplier of food to combatants that he is targeted. Now why should it matter that he would supply food whether the recipients were combatants or no? For it is not his ordinary existence and activity that are an impediment to military goals but what war makes of him – and makes of him without any changes on his part, and, indeed, without necessarily his knowledge or consent. No doubt we might more effectively remove the impediment the farmer represents by destroying his crops or his machinery. But to say this is not to exclude him absolutely, as traditional just war theory would, from those who may be targeted.

Two questions arise about the just war theory principle of discrimination understood in terms of double effect. Is its distinction between intended and merely foreseen deaths sustainable? Is there good reason for an absolute prohibition on the intentional killing of innocents? Certainly it seems hard to accept that the terrorist who places a bomb aimed at blowing up a passing army vehicle does not also intend to kill the civilians he knows will most likely be passing by. They are not killed, as in some other cases, by mistake, inadvertently or by accident: they are not killed unintentionally. Yet the terrorist has no intention or purpose to whose successful fulfilment the killing of passers-by conduces, nor does he want to kill them. In that sense he can deny that killing them was any part of what he intended. The plausibility of his denial rests, however, on the cogency of his claim to be *fighting* a war, to be engaged in *combat*. Killing ordinary civilians is no part of combat, though it is a well nigh inevitable consequence of it. But the cogency of his claim depends on two things: first, on the existence of a concept of war as a rule-governed activity by contrast with random killing and destruction: second, on the acceptance of war as that through which one's ultimate goals are to be realised, rather than through killing as such. It must often be very doubtful both whether the concept of war employed by the terrorist does conform to these requirements and whether his goals are being realised strictly with regard to them.

The difficulty of the second conception of self-defence which insists that we treat people as ends rather than means is that it cannot realistically be expected that one's ends in fighting a self-defensive war are going to correspond to the ends of those one might need to target on the enemy side, so that one might need to attack only those who are themselves *prepared* to die for their cause. This is to make of all war the sort of chivalric contest which some medieval wars maybe were, and which the no doubt necessary myths of professional soldiery make all wars to be. But certainly not all wars, and probably no modern wars, permit the observance of such chivalric codes.[12] The man who must be killed is most often the desperate conscript who would throw down his weapon and run if only he could. His ends run entirely counter to his enemy's, and each intends the death of the other solely as a means to his own security. If it is justifiable to shoot him and yet not, for the same reason, justifiable to kill whatever civilians pose a similar threat, this must presumably be because the former is prepared to treat others as means while the threat posed by the latter is not intended. Immunity is *forfeited* by those who disregard the ends of others: it is not *relinquished* by those who share each other's heroic readiness to face death.

Yet it might be doubted that any putative right to kill in self-defence is restricted to those who intend my death, and can therefore be assumed to recognise a risk of their own deaths. Others might not know how what they are doing threatens me. It is very far from clear, however, by what kind of association with the ends of those who do intend my death that others might become legitimate targets.

Conversely, those who intend my death and dig with patriotic fervour to feed the troops who encompass it surely do not thereby become legitimate targets. The fact that they might face death heroically as a risk they run for their contributing to the war effort does not make a direct attack on them any less cynical and callous. The principle of treating others as ends and not means fails to capture our intuitions as to what attacks can be allowable, confused as those intuitions may well be.

TERRORIST OUTRAGES

Public revulsion against the killing of civilians in terrorist attacks is often due to a belief that it cannot be justified on the grounds of self-defence. But this is often to assimilate two distinct ways in which the notion of self-defence can operate. In the first it serves to provide a just cause of war which may then be pursued, having due regard to the principle of discrimination. In the second it provides a reason for a particular military operation in a war. It is evident that in waging a defensive war one's opponent's political leaders may be obstacles to success, and as such may be targeted, even if they pose no threat against which a defensive operation might be mounted. They are not harmless and they intend one no good. Yet while there may be public understanding, and even exculpation, of defensive *operations* by terrorists against troops who are hunting them down, there may be

lack of understanding and outright rejection of their claim to be waging a defensive *war*. Such an assimilation would explain outrage
against terrorist attacks on civilians, such as judges and politicians,
who are targeted because they allegedly contribute to the enemy's
coercive rule. It explains too the outrage at attacks on off-duty soldiers who pose no *immediate* threat, but are, under just war theory,
legitimate targets owing to the general danger which they pose in
war.

Yet there are many other cases where outrage cannot be so
explained. Some derive from a failure or refusal to accept the dou-
ble-effect justification which the terrorist may offer. Professions of
regret at civilian casualties in pursuit of allegedly military objectives
are commonly viewed as hypocritical, as in the case of the massacre
of Enniskillen. Perhaps this is often right, and the deaths of civilians
are being directly used as a means to put pressure on politicians – as
were the deaths of the inhabitants of Hiroshima and Nagasaki.
Whether this is so depends in part on whether the terrorists are really aiming to win in war or to achieve their political goals by other
means.[13] Yet we do not show that they are not aiming at victory by
showing that they lack the *capacity* to win an outright war. They may
know that their opponents, though stronger, are unprepared for outright war: they may suspect that they will capitulate in the face of a
relatively low level of violence. A part of what will lead them to capitulate might be the scale of civilian casualties. But so long as the risk
of casualties is strictly proportionate to the goals of military operations there is no conclusive reason to think that they are being used
directly as a means to their goal.

Proportionality is the essence of defensive just war theory. Yet it is
quite unclear how a proportionate level risk to civilians in a military
operation is to be assessed. Evidently this must be related to the place
of the operation in general strategy, and that in its turn must relate
to the overall gains and losses of going to war. Thus, in general, what
ought to be regarded as acceptable civilian losses must be judged in
relation to the benefits of victory. It is arguable, for example, that the
level of collateral civilian casualties inflicted on Germany in the war
against Hitler was a small price to pay for the preservation of the
lives of innumerable civilians – socialists, homosexuals, gypsies, Jews,
Slavs and so on – who would have been doomed by an Allied
defeat.[14] But most cases are far less easy to assess and the value of life
must be measured against that of other goods. It is natural that the
assessment made by the victims should be at odds with that made by

the terrorists. Yet it is hard to see why terrorists should be less capable or willing to make an honest assessment than those engaged in conventional war even if their military weakness leads them to mount operations involving risks to civilians to which stronger forces might not need to have recourse.

Here it may be said that terrorist operations are inherently *cowardly*, that civilians' lives are put at risk simply to preserve those of the terrorists. If this charge were justified, as it no doubt often is, it would be a serious one – for it follows from the principle of double effect that one must not use the deaths of innocents to preserve one's own life. Yet that is what one would be doing if one preferred an operation which resulted in civilian deaths to one that led to the loss of one's own life on these grounds alone. But the charge as commonly levelled overlooks the fact that the former option is not preferred on these grounds alone. It is preferred because the latter carries too high a price in terms of one's capacity to carry on the war, in which one takes one's self to be justified. The problem for terrorists is precisely that their military weakness constantly forces them into the former option, while their opponents, at least ostensibly, seldom are.

If this is so, it may be concluded, the costs of terrorism are too high. If, after all, the ultimate test of proportionality depends on the benefits of victory then if a victory is unlikely its benefits, however great, will not counterbalance even small casualties to civilians. The calculation is always necessary in traditional just war theory, which holds that it is morally wrong to go to war without a probability of victory, on account of the suffering of innocent civilians that it causes. But defensive war is traditionally exempted from this requirement.[15] For here, it is felt, one has no option but to resist attack. No one could be expected to *submit* to death or servitude inevitable though it be. If this is so it provides a strong argument for certain desperate acts of terrorism – as for the uprising in the Warsaw ghetto. In doing so it makes an assessment of proportionality impossible, or practically so.

Yet surely defensive wars do not provide exemption from the requirement of a reasonable prospect of victory in every case. The justification of *necessity* has plausibility only when a direct attack is being launched or enemy occupation is a threat to life or liberty. This will seldom be the situation that terrorists face, however defensive, in a broader sense, their operations may plausibly be claimed to be. For such claims will depend upon the strength of their argument for independence, popular control or government or whatever. Such goods need careful balancing against the inevitable sufferings of war. They do not provide the justification of necessity. It would be in these cases that the terrorist justification for operations which cause civilian casualties would be most open to question.

None of this is to absolve the terrorist of war crimes. Terrorism can and certainly does include the murder or other inhumane treatment of civilian populations, which is as much a war crime if perpetrated by irregular forces in an internal conflict as by regular forces in an external one.[16] Yet there seems no good reason to think that it is a particular propensity to such crimes that counts as terrorism. To start with, not all war or warlike activity with such a tendency counts as terrorism, if by that we mean, as surely we do, what is practised by terrorists. No doubt 'obliterative war is surely terroristic',[17] so to call it terrorism may seem natural, especially if we discern no moral difference between say terror bombing from the air and car bombs. Yet, whatever their moral standing, bomber pilots can very seldom count as terrorists.[18] Nor can the other legitimate agents of the state whose openly military activities terrorise the population. Terrorism is not *open* war,[19] but its lack of openness has nothing to do with a propensity to attack civilians as opposed to any other kind of target. Those engaged in a similarly secret war against the state would be dubbed terrorists however scrupulously they conformed to the rules of war with respect to targeting protected persons.

Perhaps, though, terrorists, as their name suggests, aim to cause *terror* among civilians in a way that depends partly upon the unpredictibility of their attacks that results from the secrecy of their war.[20] Parallels in ordinary warfare will spring to mind: is not area bombing by night often designed to terrify and thereby intimidate civilians? But while terrorists have often aimed to put some groups in fear (e.g. Israeli settlers), this is not a tactic discernible in all or even most attacks involving heavy casualties amongst civilians, rather, they are designed to stretch the resources and determination of the state which has a duty to protect its civilians. Such attacks will often count as war crimes. No doubt in fact they do cause terror. The point is that there is no good argument for treating a propensity for such attacks as definitive of terrorism. Indeed my argument here has been that, in terms of just war theory principles, no reason for regarding terrorists as more immoral than those engaged in ordinary war emerges.

It is possible then to see many terrorists as operating within the very just war tradition which also explains the outrage at their campaigns; to see it, in fact, as part of a dialectic which depends precisely upon this tradition to draw attention to a cause through a resort to arms and to distinguish innocents from others. They are messages, which, of course, the state will seek to stifle. Their transmission is, in any case, clouded by the uneasy fusion of analogies that just war theory represents. But unsatisfactory as it is, just war theory does represent some shareable ground of moral discourse between the terrorist and those who suffer from his attacks. Hence it cannot be just the political inconvenience of moral outrage which the terrorist must heed, but the reasons for it which he must examine and take to heart in determining his practice.

Chapter 3

Terrorism and civil war

TERRORISM AND TYRANNICIDE

Does terrorism consist in lack of a just cause, rather than a neglect of just means? Does terrorism essentially consist in attacking people without having any right to wage a war against them at all? Certainly this would not yield a sufficient condition for terrorism: there are many wars of aggression which are not, simply as such, to be termed 'terrorist'. But it could be argued that terrorist campaigns are a specific kind of war *and* they lack a *jus ad bellum*: it is this lack which makes them terrorism, rather than, say, freedom fighting.

The view I want to look at is best presented as the denial of a certain justification for some acts of terrorism, namely that they have the same just cause as tyrannicide. The view likens terrorism to tyrannicide but denies that the just cause of tyrannicide is present. What might this just cause be? Just war theory allows that, as an external aggressor may properly be repelled by force of arms, so may a tyrant – that is to say a ruler who oppresses the people rather than acting for their good. He is not any longer to be thought of as a legitimate ruler, any more than if he had invaded the country from without. He may be justly deposed in a rebellion or, if need be, assassinated in an act of tyrannicide.

A terrorist may seem, then, to be acting like one who is seeking to defeat a tyrant or a tyrannical regime; one which oppresses the people the terrorist claims to represent. This will commonly be the justification of revolutionaries or freedom fighters. An easy response is to deny that the regime they oppose really is tyrannical, and then to deny that in actual fact they have a just cause. The terrorist's targets ought not be attacked because they are not involved in anything which warrants that response. That is, in effect, the 'one man's terrorist is another man's freedom fighter' gambit. It is, however, an unsatisfactory manoeuvre if it is intended to expose the terrorist as acting contrary to just war theory. For all that it succeeds in doing is representing him as one who endeavours to conform to it but fails, perhaps through no fault of his own apart from ignorance or idealism.

The more interesting view is rather that terrorism is *corrupt* tyrannicide, representing itself as having the justification of someone with tyrannicide's intentions, but in fact pursuing other, impermissible ends, albeit by superficially similar methods.[1] Certainly the similarity may be very great. While in external wars it may not serve the aims of war to launch attacks on the apparatus of civil government within an aggressor state, in internal terrorist campaigns it is a common, perhaps a universal feature, to attack the apparatus of civil government within the terrorist's own state. And the reason for this is that it is allegedly part of an apparatus of oppression which the terrorist is able to demolish. The question of whether terrorism is corrupt tyrannicide, and for this reason unjust, turns on whether those who are thus attacked are targeted for the right reasons or for the wrong ones.

What I here call the *corrupt tyrannicide* view of terrorism naturally goes with the view of terrorism as essentially *revolutionary*,[2] as aiming to replace a social and political structure which oppresses the people by a new order which better represents their interests. This is a largely modern conception of the role of internal anti-state violence, which, qua revolutionary, cannot be justified by just war notions. My purpose here is to see if terrorism *necessarily* fails to benefit from such a justification because it is revolutionary. Whether the more modern revolutionary conception shapes its aims or not, these older notions may still, I shall argue, have a place in our understanding of the terrorist and indeed in his own understanding of himself.

Under the two versions of just war theory which we have considered, the aim of terrorism must be either the punishment of the tyrant or defence against him. His death or, more mildly, removal from his office and all its benefits, can be seen as serving either aim. On the face of it terrorists may be seen as fulfilling either purpose. Using notions from the punitive theory the cause of *revolutionary justice*[3] is often used to explain the actions of terrorists (such as Sendero Luminoso among exploited and impoverished Peruvian peasants) in launching attacks on the agents, supporters or beneficiaries of a state they see as oppressive. The judicial system of that state is regarded as inadequate to punish acts of oppression because it is itself implicated in them. The terrorists themselves, claiming to act on behalf of the people, therefore administer the punishment deemed necessary. The objection to this account is that it rationalises an altogether less moral purpose. The terrorist's main aim, it will be said, is not to restore good government but to gain power himself. He acts, in other words, from the wrong intention, just as a state which attacks an aggressive neighbour may do if it covets some of its neighbour's territory.

Similar considerations hold if the defensive theory is applied. Claiming to defend the community against abuse of power by the regime, terrorists allegedly act to gain power for themselves. But in so doing they go beyond the proper motive for restoring peace and security to the community. Can these objections to the comparison between terrorism and tyrannicide be countered? First of all it has to be said that terrorist campaigns are very commonly waged against regimes responsible for oppressive and brutal acts. Yet equally commonly perhaps they are not – the Basques which ETA claims to represent, for instance, are not evidently oppressed. It is certainly not always possible to view terrorism as popular justice or as a defence of the community against oppression at all, and hence not as a *corrupt* form of this.

Yet when it is one of these, is it, qua terrorism, essentially corrupt? It is not easy to see why it should be so regarded. First, an ulterior motive is not as such inconsistent with having the right intentions. For example the IRA employ violence with the long-term intention of creating a united Ireland. But their immediate intention is the ending of British rule as a necessary precondition of Irish unity. If this intention serves to achieve a just cause because British rule is oppressive, then any actions arising from it are prima facie justified. It is actions over and above these which will not be.[4]

Second, while it may sometimes be right to claim that the terrorist, unlike the tyrannicide, has no interest in restoring constitutional rule, this is not always so. What is often the case is that the *form* of government under which the allegedly oppressive regime operates is held to be itself incapable of preserving the rights of the people and hence as needing to be dismantled. What is intended to be put in its place may be a new constitution, not another tyranny. That it is not the *original* constitution certainly bespeaks a difference between modern terrorism and classical tyrannicide, which harks back to an ancient constitution. But this is not a difference that renders the former a corruption of the latter. Rather it indicates a modern development whereby those who claim to act on behalf of the community in acting against a tyrant do so on the basis of a claim to popular support for their own alternative form of government, at least pending further expression of the popular will. And that is because popular sovereignty has replaced custom or natural law as a source of legitimacy for forms of government.

Third, it cannot be objected that terrorists are themselves *inherently* tyrannical in seizing power by violence. It is the motive that determines whether violence is or is not justified in the seizure of power, just as it determines whether the retention of power by force is benign or tyrannical. What is new and questionable in the case of modern terrorism is its claim to be justified in using violence against forms of oppression which are not themselves overtly violent, but, for example, economic or cultural. Yet often such questionable claims do not need to be resorted to. Terrorist attacks on what is alleged to be a regime acting out of sectional rather than public interests are commonly met with excessive force not only against the terrorist themselves, but against their supporters and the part of the population which they claim to represent. It may be hard to resist the terrorist's conclusion that the regime's behaviour confirms its own essentially violent foundations. In these circumstances the seizure of power by violence in what is held to be the public good cannot be regarded as itself tyrannical.

I conclude that the traditional just cause of tyrannicide can sometimes be offered for modern terrorism and that, in consequence, terrorism cannot be regarded as a kind of war that is unjustified because it lacks a just cause. It should be stressed, however, that this type of justification is of very limited application. The notion of 'revolutionary justice', for example, presupposes a view of the community as needing to be protected against the agents of oppressive government by the infliction of condign punishment upon them. Yet it is not clear in what circumstances, if any, this would justify a *war*, by contrast with punitive activities analogous to those of vigilantes in a poorly policed neighbourhood.

Yet this is a criticism of the admission of tyrannicide as providing a just cause for war at all; it is a criticism of this aspect of punitive just war theory rather than of its particular application to defend terrorism. Indeed it could be argued that the criticism points out the more general defect of the punitive theory, how can *war* be justified for the punishment of crime at all, when war is prosecuted by an aggrieved party rather than impartially, without any semblance of the process of law, and with terrible consequences for many more than the original malefactors?[5] There are difficulties here about the relation between war and the punishment of crime. Yet it needs to be said that if the punitive theory can provide a justification of war then its application to terrorism would be the more convincing the more closely the internal situation the terrorist confronts resembles that of external aggression. For just as aggression remains unpunished so long as occupation continues, so does an oppressive regime so long as it retains power. And then it may be the structures of government, not just the individuals they support, which need to be toppled, and that may require war.

Where recourse to war seems to be more readily justifiable is where it is viewed as defending the community against the deprivations of a tyrannical regime. Such cases do, or are taken to, arise as, they would argue, in the IRA defence of the Catholic community in the Bogside against the forces marshalled in support of the regime in Northern Ireland. Yet more commonly self-defence is viewed as mounted against an external, albeit an occupying power on behalf of a community regarded as politically distinct. In such instances it is not the just cause of tyrannicide which is principally appealed to. Yet it is worth observing that the two kinds of justification are not necessarily incompatible. Indeed in the Northern Irish case both have been offered simultaneously. But whereas attacking a tyrant is justified only by *actual* oppression, this is not required for defence against an external aggressor.

Again the underpinnings of just war theory itself invite examination here: the notion of self-defence that it employs is itself a slippery one, sliding easily, as we have seen, between defence of and by a group of individuals against injury or imprisonment or grievous loss, and defence of a community against an alien or oppressive rule. Where terrorists can persuasively claim to be engaged in the former they are on stronger ground than in the latter. For the former makes no assumption as to the identity and political legitimacy of a community to be defended – assumptions which will almost always be contradicted by their opponents. The right of a group to defend itself is at least equal to that of individuals to act collectively for this purpose. It is when a group is threatened with lawless violence by a government thereby shown to be tyrannical that the case for anti-state terrorism seems strongest.

REVOLUTIONARY STRUGGLE

Terrorism is commonly, but not invariably, revolutionary. That is to say it aims at a change in the political and social order on behalf of the political community which is thought of as oppressed under current constitutional arrangements. Although the language of the just war may be used in propaganda it may be claimed that revolutionary war involves an ideology radically at variance with it,[6] and, what is more, one that poses a serious threat to social stability.[7] If we approve it, it will be on this quite different ideological basis. If we disapprove it, it is because this ideology itself is unacceptable. Much criticism of irregular warfare and terrorism stems from the latter position. Correspondingly some defences incorporate a perhaps not fully conscious attachment to the former.

The ideological pattern involved is held to be common to many movements, whether ostensibly nationalist, socialist, religious or whatever. It involves dichotomising the *people* and their *oppressors*, represented by the state in its current form. The revolutionary group aims to act against the oppressor on behalf of the people through identifying with them and carrying forward their struggle. But in the absence of a capacity for successful popular uprising the revolutionary group must take on the superior forces of the state through means other than direct military confrontation. The victory which it intends is thus primarily political rather than military.

We have already investigated some features of this account: the ultimate political goals of the campaign and the political constraints upon the state in responding to it which are necessary for its success do not seem to rule out its being a military campaign in which military victory is sought as a means to political success. Certainly the superiority of the state's forces does not imply this. It is not only terrorists, but in many instances guerillas, who find themselves confronted with such superiority and aim to win militarily despite it. Nor does the treasonable, and hence unlawful, character of revolution deprive it of its military character: many undoubted civil wars of a quite different sort may share this feature. What is required for revolutionary war is an attack upon the state (or some organisation purporting to stand in for it if it has collapsed in civil war). That is to say a *political* organisation must be the object of attack, not just for example capitalists, Jews, whites or whoever. So long as the ideological pattern sketched makes the state essential to oppression this will always be the case. For what gives stability to the unjust status quo is precisely its underpinning by the structure of the state.

The revolutionary victory which cannot be gained by direct military means is intended to be brought about by one or other or a combination of two methods: (1) to sap the will of the forces of the state to continue fighting by a war of attrition; (2) to bring about political changes in the state resulting in the end of hostilities. The first is by no means a novel nor a modern tactic. The discipline of armies on which modern states rely is a recent phenomenon. Previously soldiers dispirited by the hardships of campaigning were relatively free to quit the ranks: tactics designed to have this result are therefore properly military. The difference in modern times is that it is likely to be the state itself which loses heart, through the demoralisation of its supporters – the contemporary equivalent of undisciplined knights and squires. The second objection, then, is, in its effect, little different from the first. But again it is hard to discern a clear distinction between it and properly military aims. Few wars are won as a result of the surrender of generals uninstructed by their governments; most by the decision of governments to negotiate some kind of peace. Military tactics will always be decided with the desirability of that in mind. So revolutionary war is aimed at persuading the supporters of the state that, in the long-term, its oppressive rule is not sustainable.

The question about the legitimacy of revolutionary war concerns whether it intends to *change* the political situation in a way that conforms to an ideological picture, or whether it simply aims to *reveal* it in that form. It is only possible to condemn it as a serious abuse of war if the former is the case. For if it is, the revolutionary will evidently lack any just cause for war. The conditions for such a cause spelled out in terms of the oppression of the people will not exist prior to the war, but will be brought about by it, through provoking the state into oppressive acts against the people. Indeed the revolutionary identification with a certain class of the population will mark this class out as 'the people' who therefore come to be oppressed. The existence of the war will produce discontent with the state authorities not previously felt, but felt now on account of their incapacity to end the war. If these tactics are deliberately embarked upon in revolutionary war then evidently it is wrong.

Yet equally evidently the ideological pattern depicts a very different scenario: the oppression of the state is a pre-existing condition which justifies revolution; the response of the state reveals its oppres-

sive character; its violent reaction towards that class of the population which harbours revolutionaries discloses its awareness of them
as a threat just because they are oppressed; expressions of discontent
indicate the growing popular awareness of this fact. If this ideological picture is to be taken seriously then it cannot be used to show that
revolutionaries have no justification for embarking on a war.

We cannot conclude then that the ideology is itself radically at
odds with just war theory. We may however wish to argue that the
ideology is radically false and thus that it cannot provide any just
cause for war. Conversely if we take the view[8] that attacks should not
be made on guerillas who have the complete support of the people,
this is likely to be because, in this instance anyway, we take their ideological picture of the situation to be accurate. It is because their
identification with the people is complete that the war 'cannot be
fought because it is no longer an anti-guerrilla but an anti-social war,
a war against an entire people, in which no distinctions will be possible in the actual fighting'. This would be to accept as accurate 'the
guerrilla's self image . . . not of a solitary fighter hiding among the
people but of a whole people mobilised for war, himself a loyal member, one among many'.[9] Yet this in itself is no reason for not attacking
them, since under just war theory, a whole people's cause may be
unjust. One will think it cannot be only if one grants at least some
truth to the ideological picture.

PROPER AUTHORITY

The gravest charge against terrorists under just war theory is that
they wage war without *proper authority*, for proper authority, along
with a just cause and right intention, is a requirement for having *jus
ad bellum*. It is necessary indeed for something properly to count as
war, for a distinction needs to be drawn between private killing –
duellum – which ordinarily counts as murder, and public killing such
as takes place in war, which ordinarily does not so count.[10] Authority,
in medieval thought, derives from a sovereign who administers the
laws. Resort to private killing in a settlement of disputes is disallowed
since such matters are to be judged by the sovereign. Yet while the
sovereign must decide on whether he has a just cause, he, unlike the
religious leader of a holy war, is in no privileged position to determine this. Nor is there any higher tribunal to judge whether he or his
adversary is in the right. What the sovereign may be expected to do,

however, is to ensure obedience to the rules for the conduct of war, since he will ultimately be responsible if they are breached.

A number of distinct notions are here brought into relation. The first is that those who fight should be under effective control, and that that control should be exercised by one who has regard for the rules of war. The only one who can be expected to have regard for the rules of war is the sovereign, for the sovereign has charge of the political community whose members are the principal beneficiaries of the observance of these rules by either side. This implies that the sovereign shall be not only a ruler, but a lawful one; for only a lawful ruler will have at heart the interest of the community, rather than his own. Thus only a sovereign should have the authority to unleash the dogs of war that inevitably bring down a degree of suffering on the community.

Stripped of the medieval assumption of the sovereign as an individual prince rather than some body corporate which represents the people, this pattern of argument still has considerable force. The initiation and control of war surely needs to be in public hands. Indeed, other things being equal, we should jib at calling the clash of private armies or armed gangs *war* in a literal sense. Armies fight wars but, as Rousseau saw,[11] it is not they but the states which employ them that are *at war*. Private armies lack the right relation to an appropriate public body to be involved in war proper: put into that relation, their clashes, otherwise unchanged, acquire this character.

The problem of proper authority for terrorists and other insurgents turns, of course, on how they might have the right relation to an appropriate public body, given that they are fighting a war against an established state. We may say that proper authority rests only with the side that has a lawful claim to the territory under dispute. Normally we should, no doubt, think this will be the state itself, troubled by vexatious and belligerent dissidents. Sometimes however the state will be usurpatious or tyrannically oppressive and forfeit its claim to exercise authority. Yet, while tempting, the equation of proper authority with a lawful claim to it should be resisted. It is significant that just war theory distinguishes proper authority from just cause as *distinct* requirements of *jus ad bellum*; were the equation correct, they would not be so, for a condition of proper authority would be an ingredient of a just cause. In the absence of further argument it is therefore prudent to acknowledge that proper authority may attach to both sides in a civil conflict just as it can in an external war, whichever's claim to the territory under dispute is the lawful one. As we shall see it is unlikely that an established state threatened by terrorists will make the same concession.

The difficulty is to decide what, in circumstances of civil strife, constitutes proper authority. There will be no doubt that an established state can normally qualify: its troops are under effective control and it has regard for the rules of war. It has charge of a political community, and shows concern for their interests. In the case of an existing state which lays claim to a larger territory it has authority because it claims a right to charge of its people and a corresponding duty of concern, shown in its actions. In the case of an occupying power it has that charge *de facto* and the rules of war lay on it the corresponding duty.[12] The difficulty rather is knowing how to assign authority to those who aspire to but do not yet possess separate statehood or the control of an existing state: 'how to distinguish brigands and gangsters from genuine revolutionaries who merit moral and legal standing'.[13]

One necessary feature must surely be that the aims of their activity are war aims; that they are intending to wage a war as a means to securing certain goals, and that these goals are the kinds of goal to which war is an appropriate means. Allowing this would not imply that revolutionaries, terrorists or insurgents generally are actually waging war, still less that they are waging the war for just ends or by just means. Rather it is the first step towards identifying their activity as different in kind, even if in its texture of violence it looks indistinguishable, from brigandry or gangsterism.

Consider the Greek Klefts who terrorised parts of Greece under the Ottoman Empire.[14] Their acts of violence, pillage and hostage-taking were part of a war of national liberation and would, in modern times, count as terrorism. After the inauguration of an independent Greek monarchy, however, the Klefts continued their activities, becoming as one might say *mere* brigands. How did this change of circumstances lead to their no longer counting as terrorists? It is too loose to say that they no longer had a political motive (the ingredient which turns the use of violence into terrorism according to such legal definitions as occur in British Prevention of Terrorism legislation). Certainly an overriding political motive is necessary – the Mafia are not terrorists, although they are involved in political intrigue and assassination, because their ultimate ends are private ones. In fact the Klefts continued to act for political motives involving the pursuit of factional ends; but even this is insufficient for terrorism. A bank robber who contributes his haul to party funds is not thereby a terrorist, even though terrorism can include bank raids. Nor can we hold simply that a terrorist act is *expressive* of political dissent or is a political *act*. Riots in which property is destroyed or people killed can be political expressions, but seldom, if ever, terrorist acts. They may be, however, if the crowd takes up arms in a *levée en masse*. And here again the same factor that is required for terrorism is present: the intention to wage a war.

Not every group that takes up arms with the intention of waging war has the proper authority to do so. But the intention is, I suggest, sufficient for regarding such groups within the state as insurgents, of which terrorist groups are a species. The intention is possible only for a group which seeks political control of the state or of some of its territory. A 'genuine' revolutionary movement will seek such control on the basis of the claim to act on behalf of a political community. Such a claim is a further condition of proper authority for waging war. Without it the contender for power has no motive for acting to protect the community in it through war.

It may seem now that we must decide which groups that *claim* to act on behalf of a community are *really* doing so. There are many pitfalls in this formulation. First we should be ill-advised to decide in advance of acknowledging proper authority what the communities to be represented are, for commonly in civil strife the parties to the conflict will disagree over what are the relevant communities. If they agree on this, and each claims to represent one or another community, then the war will be more like external conflict concerned only with staking out territorial boundaries for each community. In that case acknowledging proper authority will not be difficult. But, second, if more than one group claims to represent a single community we should not confuse the issue of which of them, either or both, has authority with questions about which has *support*.[15] This would mean taking a particular political stance on what *justifies* a claim of acting on behalf of a community. But it is one thing to act on behalf of someone or some community and another to act on their behalf as of right. Someone may act on an absent neighbour's behalf by having his or her sick dog put down yet act, in all probability, without any right. Thus, third, we should not confuse the political question of who in fact acts in a community's interest with the question of who honestly believes themselves to be doing so. The latter is necessary for making plausible a claim to be acting on another's behalf. It demands a preparedness to forego one's own private interest in pursuit of the interest of those on whose behalf one claims to act. This seems to be an essential condition for having proper authority, capturing the relationship of service to a community required of its leaders.

What we have not yet fully captured, however, is the essentially public character required for them to have proper authority. For that, the interests of those whom the group represents must be political interests, and the group must further them by political means. This is intended not to contrast with military means but to indicate that the military must be employed under *political* control. The cowboys who, in old movies, organise Mexican peasants to defend themselves against predatory landlords intend to wage a war; they may have political motives, including that of seeking a degree of political autonomy for the peasants; they may act on their behalf, contrary to their own interests; but they unquestionably lack proper authority to wage a war. And this is because they do not themselves fall under political control: their ragged army as yet lacks a political existence. The conditions for a group to count as political and hence to be able to exercise political control are certainly unclear, but at the very least it has to have a conception of the intended peacetime shape and structure of the political community, whether this is in terms of the restitution of an old constitution or the introduction of a new one; and it must view itself as the instrument for realising this conception.

How does this discussion of the nature of proper authority bear on the question of whether or when we should concede proper authority to insurgent groups? We can classify a number of different types of group depending upon their conception of the political community they claim to represent and their consequent view of their own role in relation to it. (1) *Conservative* groups are those that seek to preserve or restore political arrangements against the threat of change. The community is identified through such constitutional arrangements. Characteristically these groups will consist of elements of the governing class and its military supporters. The key question to ask about such a group will be whether it genuinely has at heart the interests of the wider community rather than only its own sectional interests. (2) *Democratic* groups claim to act on behalf of the community in virtue of popular support within it. The community is shaped by popular consent to particular democratic procedures. The group will typically consist of politically disadvantaged parts of the community. Here the question will be whether the facts about support, as known to the group, make their claim credible. (3) *Vanguardist* groups avow concern for the real interests of the community, previously unrepresented, whether or not the community itself grasps the nature of its own real interests. The community is identified in terms of its members' common interests. The group will often be drawn from economically and socially disadvantaged sections or their sympathisers. The questions to raise here will concern the genuinely *political* character of the interests represented and the existence of political control. (4) *Patriotic* groups aim to make secure the 'real' identity of the community on the basis of features other than those mentioned above, but typically homeland, history, culture or race. Here we can ask whether the group is acting on behalf of people who make up a community, and in their interests, rather than simply in pursuit of an idea about how people *should* be grouped.

This typology is crude and incomplete. It is however designed to relate the question of proper authority for insurgent groups to their own political objectives, without begging too many questions as to the reasonableness of their aims. Although the nomenclature adopted suggests connections with distinctions as between right-wing and left-wing political conceptions, this is a merely contingent connection. Each of the types of group mentioned could be of the right or the left in terms of their peacetime policies, just as the state they oppose could be: it is a serious mistake to think of insurgent groups solely in terms of *revolutionary* politics as understood on the left. Nor are the types clearly discrete. Combinations or confusions of types can and do occur. They are merely at best convenient idealisations. We turn next to a closer scrutiny of insurgency, and its relation to 'normal' warfare.

IRREGULAR WAR

Two features of insurgency must be distinguished. First it is an ingredient in a *civil* war, though not all civil wars involve insurgency. In some cases no obvious state and anti-state sides are discernible, but, for instance, two factions within the state's forces fight for supremacy. Second, insurgency typically, though not invariably, involves *irregular* war, that is to say attacks by forces not ordinarily part of the forces of the state. Such forces may dissolve and re-form for ambushes and small-scale engagements which do not expose them to easy defeat as a result of their relative weakness in men or material. Engagements of this sort constitute *guerilla* tactics. They are a typical, though not invariable, feature of irregular war, because irregular war is typically conducted against a state with stronger forces.

It is a key distinction between regular and irregular soldiers that the military identity of the former is, in general, open and unconcealed, that of the latter hidden and secret.[16] The distinction, as I am drawing it, relates to knowledge of a soldier's military identity *outside* the context of actual military engagements. No doubt there are many regular soldiers who because of their activities in 'under-cover' operations are known to be soldiers only to their immediate families and friends. But these are an exception, just as it is an exception to the general rule that the leaders of irregular forces are widely known.

The secrecy of irregular forces is a matter of degree, depending in large part on the risks of openness. The identity of guerrillas will be known inside, but not outside some small tight-knit village communities: in cities, terrorist cells can remain entirely hidden. Typically the risks of disclosure will involve the danger of detention or death at the hands of the police or troops of the state; in other cases, at the hands of opposing irregular forces. In the typical case the motive for secrecy is relative weakness; in others the stealth of the opposing side. Yet whatever its motive the secrecy of irregular forces contributes strongly to an atmosphere of uneasiness and apprehension in civil strife. It is part of a more general atmosphere of uncertainty as to the actions and attitudes of others. It is not, it seems, intolerable that some of one's fellows should engage in acts of horrifying violence. Regular soldiers well known in the community do that. What is intolerable is that one's neighbours should do it unknown to one.

I wish to set irregular warfare within a general context of fear arising from secrecy itself. It is fear arising not only from what the terrorists or other irregulars in one's neighbourhood may do, but from the suffering that may ensue from what is done to them. This fear has two aspects, which I shall consider in reverse order. The first is a prudential fear of the consequences of living among those militarily opposed to the state. The second is a moral fear of having no adequate resources of rationality and resolve to deal with this situation. The moral problem arises from the fact that in the circumstances envisaged one can no longer be an *ordinary* citizen. The price of *secret* war is the loss of the citizen's *privacy*. She may at any time have to declare her allegiance to one side or the other, and the costs of her declaration for herself, her family and friends may be very high. This is a situation characteristic of terror, as it is visited upon civilians, whether – perhaps unavoidably – in civil strife, or as a deliberate instrument of state policy. What is the nature of the citizen's unease in this situation? Why is it so frightening? Why do we regard it as a situation which should not be deliberately produced? The uneasiness is not, I suggest, merely that occasioned by fear of the consequences of opting for what is, in prudential terms, the wrong side. Ordinary people can, without being heroic, come to terms with the consequences of loyalties they have espoused without pressure. What is horrifying is being forced by deliberate pressure or the pressure of circumstance to espouse a cause that exposes one to risks. And this is partly because calculations of the risk cannot be absent from one's mind in deciding one's loyalties. We are not choosing them freely; and insofar as our choices determine our identities – as, of necessity, they will in a situation where it is impossible to be detached – then our identities are no longer fully our own. We fear the loss of control that threatens our capacity to make any rational choices or to display any resolve. We fear the loss of a moral identity.[17]

Our loathing of deliberately induced terror is a loathing of this kind of treatment of people. For it, far more than any other, treats them merely as means, denying them even the dignity of dying for a cause in denying them the voluntary espousal of one. Yet who is to bear the responsibility for such a morally squalid situation? Is it the guerillas who shelter among ordinary citizens? Or is it the state that responds in a way that puts its citizens at risk unless they disarm the guerillas? The question is one we also need to ask about the physical suffering of citizens caught up in this scenario, of which they have a proper prudential fear.

Guerilla fighters do not violate the rules of war through living as and among ordinary citizens when not fighting. They violate the rules only if they pose as ordinary citizens when fighting, i.e. do not wear uniforms and carry weapons openly as is required of belligerents. The distinction is an important one, since it is often thought that it is this violation which puts citizens at risk.[18] It would do so only if the guerrillas were fighting among ordinary citizens, as well as living among them. Then the opposing forces would be unable to distinguish legitimate from illegitimate targets, and civilians would be liable to be mistaken for guerrillas or to be shot at in case they were. But this is not the danger that civilians are routinely exposed to by the presence of guerrillas among them. Rather the danger is that they should be killed or injured in counter-insurgency operations: either in the course of 'search and destroy' missions mounted against guerrilla bases by ground forces or as a result of tactics designed to deny the guerrillas their sanctuary through shelling and bombing. An attendant danger is that of imprisonment either by way of internment of all those who might be guerrillas or their militarily active supporters, or by way of clearing 'free fire' zones through separating civilians from combatants.

It is commonly held that guerrillas bear responsibility for the suffering of civilians in these circumstances.[19] It is the guerrillas who deliberately obscure the distinction between combatant and noncombatant so that this distinction cannot easily be observed in the opponent's response. But why should the tempter be blamed for the offence, and not the offender? And what precisely is the difference between the guerrillas' behaviour here and that of ordinary troops?

To take this last question first. It is contrary to the rules of war deliberately to use the immunity of civilians as a cover for attack, e.g. by siting a machine gun nest next to a hospital. Indeed troops have a responsibility to evacuate civilians from their military positions. But, to repeat, this is not the kind of danger to civilians for which guerrillas are principally responsible, which is simply the danger of living amongst them. Regular troops occupy camps in the vicinity of cities; their command posts, arsenals and supply stores are similarly located; so too are their munitions factories and the like. Were these to be attacked civilians would probably be killed and injured, and certainly so if the attacks involved shelling or bombing. The distinguishability of troops and civilians is salient only with respect to a particular form of attack. High-flying bombers are unable reliably to distinguish civilian from military targets. With respect to such attacks the behaviour of ordinary troops is no different from that of guerrillas. And it is probably from such attacks that civilians living in the vicinity of guerrillas have most to fear. The dangers stemming from their indistinguishability at close quarters are great only in proportion to the state's preparedness to commit ground troops against the guerrillas. Then, as has often been observed,[20] the problem of immediate indistinguishability can commonly be overcome by discriminating methods akin to police work.

Turning then to the first question of where responsibility lies for harm to civilians in guerrilla areas: if the state cannot command the discipline required for discriminating methods, then it cannot escape some responsibility for the indiscriminate behaviour of its troops, even if they are provoked. To pretend otherwise is simply to make a morally acceptable resort to war impossible, except for the state or for regular forces in a disintegrating state. For those opposed to the state will normally lack the resources to put regular troops into the field and to supply them there. Opposition forces will frequently need to be part-time soldiers supporting themselves in civilian occupations or relying on the direct support of civilian sympathisers. The state's claim that they are responsible for the suffering their presence brings down upon those civilians smacks of intimidation, rather than serious moral appraisal.

Perhaps however a guerrilla war should not be fought at all if this is the likely reaction of the state and these are the consequences. Very likely it should not. But by the same token there would be few modern wars that should be fought, in view of the proximity and indistinguishability of civilian and military targets with respect to aerial bombardment or submarine attacks.[21] Civilians are put at risk whenever war is undertaken against an adversary armed with such weaponry. But here the state simply accepts that they will come under at least indirect attack and assumes responsibility for it. If the proportion of civilian to military losses is less in these conventional conflicts than in guerrilla wars, then this may well be referable to a state's greater fear of retaliation from strong conventional forces than from weak guerillas, rather than to factors inherent in guerrilla warfare itself. In any case the high level of civilian casualties in guerrilla wars indicates that the guerrilla is unable to rely on non-combatant immunity for his own protection. The charge[22] that he relies on non-combatant immunity but thereby undermines it seems, therefore, unjustified. It must be assumed that he makes the same calculation of proportion in his military tactics as other forces do.

The prudential fear of citizens caught up in irregular warfare is fully justified. Yet it need have no sounder basis than similar fears in conventional war. No general proscription of guerrilla war can, so far as I can see, be supported on the strength of it.

CIVIL STRIFE

Terrorism *terrifies*. Whatever the justice of the terrorist's cause, whatever his methods, whether arousing terror is his aim or not, the terrorist campaign of violence does terrify. This in itself can appear as a reason for waging a 'war against terrorism' rather than against the terrorists themselves. What is the nature of this apprehension and how reasonable is it? Is this response justified?

It has been said that:

The main point about terrorism is this: every political community has understood that random and indiscriminate violence is the ultimate threat to social cohesion and thus every community has some form of prohibition against it. Terrorism allowed full sway would reduce civil society to the state of nature where there is Hobbes's fine description, 'continual fear of violent death and the life of man, poor, nasty, brutish and short'. No political society can sanction terrorism, for that would be a self-contradiction, as the very reasons for entering civil society were to escape precisely those conditions imposed by the terrorist.[23]

Writing of this 'warre of every man against every man' Thomas Hobbes himself noted:

It may peradventure be thought, there was never such a time, nor condition of warre as this: and I believe it was never generally so, over all the world, but there are many places, where they live so now. For the savage people in many places of *America*, except the government of small families, the concord whereof dependeth on naturall lust, have no government at all; and live at this day in that brutish manner, as I said before. How so ever, it may be perceived what manner of life there would be, where there were no common power to feare: by the manner of life, which men that have formerly lived under a peacefull government, use to degenerate into, in a civill war.[24]

Hobbes's evocation of Red Indian savagery excites a potent image of the horrors of civil strife into which we fall when loosed from the restraints of civilised rule. It is of course highly misleading. Indian wars had the character of external, not civil, conflicts dependent upon the internal unity and authority of tribes. Yet of course civil conflicts do occur and when they do they are commonly brutal and always fearful. Thus it is suggested that the only way to convince someone who doubts Hobbes's demand for a 'common power to fear' is to

live in a country where authority has disappeared . . . he will soon discover the meaning and prescience of Hobbes's gloomy imaginings. I lived for a month in Ireland in 1922. There was no actual loss of life near us during that time, only a few shots audible in the night. Yet there was fear and suspicion everywhere and all peaceful avocations had come to an end. Fear and veiled hostility had destroyed the whole structure of social life.[25]

Both of the commentators quoted accept Hobbes's picture of a 'war of every man against every man', first as correctly characterising the state of civil strife exemplified by terrorism; second as the inevitable result of the absence of 'a common power'. But it is evident, first, that in civil strife there are generally two sides, each under the control of some authority, rather than as many sides as there are individuals, each warring against the other. Second it is highly contestable whether the Hobbesian picture of degeneration into civil strife as inevitable in the absence of a common authority is justified by the evidence. Perhaps it is only highly likely in certain sorts of society. There is a major difference here, which we shall need to investigate later, between the Hobbesian picture of the state of nature as discordant and violent and the medieval one which sees man's natural state as social and peaceable. What is common to both however is a keen apprehension of the ills of civil strife and the need for structures of authority to avert it.

So far however we have found no argument for the forcible suppression of insurgency on the grounds that, whatever the justice of its cause, it is inherently uncontrollable because it lacks proper authority and hence leads to violent anarchy. In any event a state campaign against insurgency, a war against terrorism, is itself a form of civil strife, not the prevention of it. It is the nature of the campaign, not the fact of it, that will determine whether civil strife is persistent or curtailed.

The fact is that the defence of society itself and the protection of citizens are invariably used as a justification for the state to subdue violent opposition, without troubling too much with the insurgent's cause. We shall later look at the state's grounds for acting in this way. What we must now turn to is some tentative investigation of civil war, in an attempt to determine from whence the particular horror of it derives.

Civil wars are of several different sorts. We may distinguish first those wars in which one party is the state from those in which neither party is recognisable as such. (For simplicity we shall consider only civil wars between *two* opposing forces.) Second, we may distinguish those in which both sides recognise the same political community or communities from those in which the identification of the community or communities is in dispute. Third, we may distinguish those in which boundaries are agreed from those in which they are not. And fourth, we distinguish wars which are in the main conventional from those which, on one or both sides, involve irregular warfare. These distinctions will yield, without any further sub-divisions, twelve prima facie possible types of civil war (the case of agreed boundaries and disputed communities being ruled out). And we can see immediately that some are quite different in character from others. For example, a war which, although neither party recognisably represents the pre-existing state, is fought on conventional grounds to establish the boundaries of two new states whose communities are identified and agreed upon, has very much the character of an external war between two existing states engaged in a territorial dispute. By contrast a revolutionary war fought by irregulars to replace the existing state structure has a quite different character. It would be surprising, then, if the horror of civil war could be put down to a single source. I shall look at only two, since the terrors of irregular warfare itself have already been dwelt upon, and territorial disputes in themselves lack a civil dimension.

Civil war in which the state is under attack by revolutionary irregulars and in which irregular armies are battling for control of the state is deeply troubling, wherever one's sympathies lie. The state, except in extremes of tyranny or weakness, provides a degree of security for its citizens to carry on their ordinary lives free from the depredations of criminals. That office can be fulfilled fairly effectively by the regular armies of occupying powers too, and in just the same way by both sides in a conventional civil war, except in the immediate vicinity of the battle lines where war itself makes ordinary life impossible. But in irregular war there are no clear battle lines. When war is waged in an area lying between the undisputed lands of two communities it may have little impact elsewhere. But where two irregular forces or irregulars and the state both claim to represent the same community it is the whole country that is disputed between them. While conventional troops hold territory within which the security of citizens can be maintained, irregular forces lack the capacity to do so: it is this that forces them into evasive tactics. And under pressure from irregulars the hold of conventional troops is weakened, often to the extent that they retreat to secure bases or resort to evasive tactics themselves. In these circumstances the ordinary security of citizens disappears. Ordinary life is disrupted by the conduct of war and even where it can continue is threatened by unchecked crime.

It is cases such as these, I suggest, that give rise to 'Hobbes's gloomy imaginings', imaginings which dwell in particular on the insecurity that stems from vulnerability to crime rather than upon the risks of hunger and disease that spring from the breakdown of social and economic life in a war zone. And perhaps as a result of the force of Hobbes's picture, it is the former kind of insecurity that still haunts our imagination when confronted with situations of civil strife. In the Somalian famine of 1992, produced by the disruption of irregular civil war, it was the fact that the rice distributed by relief agencies was liable to be stolen at gun point that particularly troubled reporters, rather than the absence of food in the first place. Yet it is the risk of famine and epidemic that holds the greatest danger. It may however be the easiest to accept; partly because it seems to be a natural evil rather than one caused by men, and partly because it is an apparent consequence of the fighting of war itself rather than a result of the vacuum of power that the war creates – something especially troubling in civil strife.

The apprehension that lack of 'a common power' – a power for oneself and others to fear – engenders is not of being defenceless. One may or may not be so. The apprehension arises from *having* to defend oneself, successfully or otherwise. That does lead, as Hobbes's commentators observe, to a replacement of mutual trust by mutual suspicion which makes ordinary social intercourse impossible. It is the security of trusting one's fellows, even in times of terrible hardship that disappears.

Yet there are cases, in the sorts of civil war in which its loss is most to be feared, where that security survives. Close-knit village societies, like those in Vietnam for example, did not fall apart in this way despite the guerrilla war that was waged among them. In this case, it appears, 'a common power to fear' was not quite necessary for security. This observation brings us directly to the second kind of horror that civil war can bring.

Distinct from the loss of a common power is the loss of a clearly identifiable political community. It is this that may occur in those civil wars originating in disputes over whether one or more separate communities are to be discerned within a particular territory, typically in secessionist conflicts.

Two cases need to be distinguished here. In one the secessionists are sure of their own distinctiveness from others and the grounds of this distinctiveness are readily recognisable to them. The inter-penetration of members of what are seen as two communities creates dangers for both; dangers from attempts at forcible exclusion from a new state or forcible integration into the old one, or, failing either, of ruthless killings on both sides. This can happen in *any* civil war, whether the identification of communities is or is not at issue. But it is where it is the issue that this consequence is particularly likely, since, where it is not, shared recognition of membership of the same political community can serve to check the persecution of the enemy's sympathisers: they must, after all, eventually be brought under the same rule, unless they are to be destroyed completely. Exile, for example, is not an option. And that fact too may check the actions of the non-secessionist side, while nothing comparable can weigh with the secessionists. These are dangers that result from the fact that the secessionists have made it clear that they are unprepared, at least for the present, to live as members of a single community within the original state. That fact alone can destroy whatever community there might have been. Each side in the conflict may, however, be confident of its members' solidarity and enjoy the society which it makes possible.

The other case – and of course there are innumerable transitional ones – is that in which there are no such certainties and no evident grounds of difference. In these cases the citizen may or may not know where his loyalties lie. But whether he does or not he is unlikely to know fully where his neighbours' loyalties lie. Mistrust will make the ordinary functioning of a single community impossible until the issue is resolved. Someone may be viewed correctly or mistakenly as sympathising with the enemy, and suffer persecution, exile, or isolation in consequence. But in addition to these concrete anxieties, there are other equally real if less tangible ones. If people cannot agree on the question of which community they belong to then those social relations between them that depend on shared membership of the community will no longer be possible – except where they may persist unselfconsciously. The fear here is of loss of human society. But now it is the loss itself, rather than the insecurity resulting from it, that is the object of one's fear.

The contrast should not be too sharply drawn. Certainly without a degree of security human society becomes impossible. But the social isolation of the individual who is unsure in principle what larger society he might look to for mutuality of trust is different in theory if not in fact from the personal isolation of one who, for good practical reasons, does not know in whom he may place his trust. The conceptions that shape such anxieties remain obscure. We should be unwise to pass them off, like Hobbes, as referable to human nature, rather than to a nature shaped by human history and society itself.

Chapter 4

Terrorism and political crime

THE STATUS OF TERRORISM

The unjust war model regards terrorists as a kind of criminal, namely war criminals – guilty of war crimes for injustice in war or of crimes against peace for unjustly going to war. But this presupposes that they are fighting *in a war*, or are to be so treated, and that may be disputed. Are they irregular *soldiers* at all, or only common *criminals* – albeit criminals with a political motivation similar to that which soldiers might have for enlisting? It is this latter view, the *political crime* model of terrorism, as I shall call it, which we shall shortly investigate. But first we need to look at the case for denying that terrorists are engaged in war at all.

Two aspects of this case have already been discussed: one is that terrorists really have political aims not necessarily to be achieved through attaining the proper aims of war, namely military victory, but by violence unrelated to attaining that aim; the other is that terrorists lack the proper authority required for fighting a war, and instead are engaging in private violence. We found neither of these objections conclusive. Both depend, furthermore, on the just war conception of war, and this itself, as we shall shortly see, may be disputed. Meanwhile two further aspects of the case may be mentioned: first, that terrorists actually operate in *peacetime* and deliberately avoid attracting a military response; second, that what constitutes war is determined by the law, and under it terrorism does not count as waging war.

This first objection will collapse into the second if a legal criterion for what constitutes war, and therefore peacetime, is employed. Perhaps it need not be. Perhaps we can agree that if terrorists, such as the Red Brigades or the RAF, manage to mount only a few sporadic attacks to which states do not need to make a military response then no war exists, whatever they claim to the contrary. But this is only one kind of case at the extreme end of a spectrum of mounting violence. At the other extreme peace no longer exists, whatever the state claims to the contrary. The reason for this is that while terrorists have the intention to wage war, they may lack the capacity in varying degrees.

Is it really the case though that when terrorists mount their attacks from a position of weakness they are then intending to wage war? Even if they understand that their capacity is too limited for war they may intend that the attacks they launch should become part of a war if they eventually gain that capacity. In this sense they intend to wage a war. For if they succeed, those early attacks will then count as the war's first engagements; their intention to wage a war does not come later. What may come later – and what it is possible to confuse with the intention to wage a war – is a willingness to elicit a military response. But to be unwilling to elicit this is quite consistent with intending to wage war. It is simply a stratagem which may, at least in certain circumstances, be explained by the desire to conserve resources or recruit support for later stages in a possible campaign. As such it is regularly resorted to at the outset of conventional wars, where provocative but minor acts of aggression announce hostile intentions which may later lead to outright war, or, alternatively, to negotiations – an outcome that terrorists also would sometimes prefer to war, just as others do who intend to go to war in the absence of a negotiated settlement.

The avoidance of attracting a military response by terrorists is partly, as the foregoing suggests, a political ploy. It depends upon an assessment of the political costs to the enemy of making an overly overt military response or maintaining a posture of impregnability. It may also be a military tactic – an extreme instance of the war of evasion practised by guerrillas. If terrorists are very well concealed among a civil population then a discriminating military response, even if recommendable, may be impossible. The success of terrorists in such manoeuvres does nothing to show that they are not really waging war. I conclude once again therefore that this further objection to the view that terrorists are engaged in war does not stand up to scrutiny.

The final objection to be considered – that terrorists are not *in law* waging a war – requires some stage setting. It hinges on a quite different conception of war from that offered by a just war theory. The contrasting conception may be termed the *positivist* one.[1] Positivism, in this connection, may be characterised as the theory that social phenomena, such as war or terrorism, are characterised in terms of the rules in force which regulate or prohibit them. These rules are not – as they are in just war theory – *moral* rules, in principle accessible to anyone who is capable of the appropriate insights vouchsafed by natural or by divine law. We can contrast these with the *positive* laws enforced by particular states or the international system – even though positive laws may be influenced by moral beliefs. Notoriously ignorance of the law is no excuse. This is not because we are expected to have knowledge of it through consulting our own consciences. Rather it is a failure to consult a solicitor in appropriate circumstances that is not excused, for legal advice may be needed to discover what the state of the law is on a given question. For positivism it is positive laws which constitute the rules that characterise very many social phenomena, including war. What counts as war is determined by the laws of the land and international law.

A word should be said about international law. Under positivism the state may make what laws it will; but what gives them the force of law is the existence of sanctions upon law breaking. International law, by contrast – and contrary to the impression sometimes given by powerful states – is not made by superpowers which impose sanctions upon those states that break it. It should be mentioned that it is not a fear of such sanctions, often impossible to enforce, that by and large secures compliance. Rather international laws, for example of war, codify existing usages which states have found it in their interests to pursue. The fact that it is established *states* whose customs and consent determine international law has considerable significance.

Thus it is between existing states that international law treats war as paradigmatically waged; for the provisions of international law relate almost exclusively to inter-state conflicts. This is not surprising since, as we have seen, international law is fundamentally concerned with the behaviour of states (although it can be applied to individuals, as in the case of war crimes). Insofar as international law recognises internal conflict as war it does so principally in connection with such questions as whether intervention is permissible by a third party, namely another state. Such cases must of necessity be rare; for the general principle of non-intervention in the internal affairs of another state is required to create a distinction between those matters that are subject to international law and those that are properly and exclusively the concern of a state's domestic law. No state will consent to international law that tends to undermine its sole prerogative to see to its own internal affairs. Any right of outside intervention that is conceded must therefore be expected to enhance the authority of existing states rather than to diminish it.

Three grounds for permissible military intervention by one state within the boundaries of another may be discerned,[2] one of which, the right of humanitarian intervention to protect citizens exposed to massacre, typically at the hands of their own government, is not our present concern. The others deal with intervention on behalf of a secessionist minority or counter-intervention against a state which has already intervened in such a conflict. Both of these allowable cases can be regarded as conferring the status of war on an *internal* conflict through the permissibility of it becoming an *international* one, but they are strictly limited: in particular the first normally requires that the secessionist struggle is sustained, general, and sufficiently successful for insurgents to occupy and administer a substantial part of the state's territory, or at the least to control it to such an extent as to enable them to carry out concerted military operations in accordance with the rules of war.[3] It is clear that by these tests terrorists will almost always fail to count as insurgents who can be regarded as fighting a war. Their struggle may be erratic, far from general, characterised by evasive rather than conventional military confrontations and hence unsuited to gaining territory.

By this kind of criterion, if the terrorists are not secessionists they do not even begin to qualify for recognition as engaged in war. However, recent international law[4] confers a general recognition on 'armed conflicts in which people are fighting against colonial domination and alien occupation and against racist regimes in exercise of their right of self determination'. While this may cover some terrorist groups (e.g. in South Africa) it evidently excludes many others and appears not to apply to struggles by secessionist minorities to partition existing states. It should further be noted that it is doubtful whether terrorists can always be regarded as engaged in 'armed conflict' since this has been held to imply 'a certain kind of intensity of military operations' which terrorists may well fall below – 'isolated and sporadic acts of violence' are specifically excluded. Indeed jurists suggest that the level must be such as to oblige the state which is attacked to resort to military force against the insurgents. Simply by declining to do so the state can prevent recognition under international law that terrorists are engaged in warfare.

This points up the most important consequence of the positivist picture. It is that, in the majority of cases, it is the state attacked which determines whether terrorists are to be regarded as waging war or not. This can be seen most vividly from the fact that insurgents may be accorded belligerent status and hence given the rights of prisoners of war under the Geneva Conventions on certain conditions – namely that they are under responsible command, wear some distinctive sign or uniform, carry arms openly and operate in accordance with the rules of war.[5] Even in the rare cases where these conditions are satisfied by a terrorist group, however, nothing *obliges* a state to treat them as belligerents in an *internal*, by contrast with an *international*, conflict. It may simply suit the state's political purposes not to do so. If we accept the positivist conception of war then the rejection of belligerent status to terrorists is impossible to resist. We shall shortly investigate the strength of the grounds for its acceptance. But if terrorists are not waging war how are they to be regarded?

TERRORISM AS CRIME

On the face of it terrorists are simply common criminals, guilty of acts of murder, grievous bodily harm, arson, criminal damage and so forth. For if they were to be accorded belligerent status at least some of their acts would not count as criminal, since the principal point of such recognition is precisely to exempt acts that would otherwise be contrary to domestic law. It should be remembered however that acts contrary to the rules of war – even if they attract further condemnation as war crimes – count as breaches of domestic law: deliberate killing of civilians is murder, burning down their houses arson and so forth. Refusal to accord belligerent status simply puts the killing of soldiers and the bombing of their barracks on the same footing as attacks upon civilians and civilian property.

Yet despite their constant insistence that terrorists are simply common criminals, states seldom consistently treat them as such. To the extent that they do *not*, a positivist conception of their *peculiar* character becomes possible. Consider by way of an example the United Kingdom government's treatment of Irish Republican (and indeed Loyalist) terrorists.[6] In Britain there is Prevention of Terrorism legislation which allows the police wider than usual powers to detain suspects for questioning if a violent offence is thought to be terrorist – that is to say, committed for political ends. In Northern Ireland, under emergency legislation, the courts that try alleged terrorist offences are constituted differently and with different rules of evidence from ordinary courts. Furthermore, despite some changes of policy, Republican prisoners in Ireland have been granted concessions concerning prison conditions which, government protestations to the contrary notwithstanding, confer a special and essentially political status on them.

Under the legislation alluded to, several Republican and Loyalist organisations are proscribed so that mere membership of them is an offence. The grounds for proscription are explicitly or implicitly that they are 'concerned in terrorism or in promoting or encouraging it'. It is evident that a special category of crime is here conceded. And in the past states have always made such a concession in what they deemed their national interests. The extradition of criminals who flee the country has traditionally excluded criminals with political motives. The reason for this has been that extradition of political offenders is taken to be interference in the domestic affairs of another state: it is not up to a state to influence the political developments of another in this way.[7]

More recently, however, terrorists have been specifically excluded from the political offence exclusion to extradition, for example through the incorporation of the European Convention on the Suppression of Terrorism into the extradition laws of the EC states.[8] This Convention stipulates that immunity from extradition cannot be granted on political grounds for a number of offences including hijacking, hostage-taking and bombing or participation in attempts at these crimes. The list is intended to cover those offences which, with the addition of a political motive, would be terrorist. Paradoxically the attempt to deprive terrorists of the benefit of their political status serves to highlight it further, and to mark out more precisely a legal category of terrorism.

What I am calling the political crime model of terrorism attempts to specify this category in such terms as 'the resort to violence for political ends by unauthorised non-governmental actors in breach of accepted codes of behaviour regarding the expression of dissatisfaction with, or dissent from or opposition to the pursuit of political goals by the legitimate government authorities of the state whom they regard as unresponsive to the needs of certain groups of people'.[9] The notion of *violence* employed here is evidently one which implies the commission of crimes contrary to such legislation as that against murder, kidnapping and so forth.

For a correct understanding of the political crime model this feature of what makes terrorist acts criminal needs to be stressed. Those who espouse the model affirm that 'terrorist acts . . . constitute criminal rather than political offences, and should be prosecuted as such'.[10]

The contrast here is between those offences for the *commission* of which the question of political motivation is irrelevant, and those for which a political motive is required. All states have laws against political offences such as treason (which in Britain under an Act of 1351 makes it a capital offence to 'levy war against our Lord the King in his realm'). But these offences, though they may be committed in conjunction with ordinary criminal offences like murder, are separable from them. The political crime model locates the *criminal* character of terrorism outside of its political motivation. And this reflects the state's disinclination to try terrorists for treason or other political offences. If it did then the question of the political justification of terrorist acts would be raised. It is important for the state to insist that no question of justification can be raised: terrorist acts, though politically motivated, are to be regarded as never politically justified because they are merely criminal.

Terrorists break the 'accepted codes of behaviour' in pursuit of their political ends. Here then is a further system of rules in relation to which terrorism is defined, namely rules for advancing political causes. In liberal democracies these prescribe the support of candidates for an elected government, or for an assembly from which government is drawn and to which it is responsible. In such societies, it is implied, there is no justification for pursuing political ends by other means and, a fortiori, not by *violent* means. In other societies there may be no adequate channels for expressing opposition to the legitimate government, or even nothing that can be recognised as a legitimate government at all.

For these cases the political crime model does not recognise anything as terrorism. The notion has a clear application only within a certain kind of political system. Elsewhere we recognise rebels, assassins, saboteurs and so forth engaged in just the same criminal acts as terrorists and with similar political motives. But their acts, which will also count as a species of political crime, may in the circumstances be justified. They do not count as terrorism, whatever their governments may say, not because they *are* justified – as in the view that your terrorist is my freedom fighter – but just because, against the different institutional background of, for example, a totalitarian state, they *may* be justified.

The political crime model captures a good deal of ordinary everyday thinking about terrorism. It does so no doubt because it is the model that derives from the preferred practice of Western governments, and is thereby surreptitiously disseminated in their identification and condemnation of terrorists. This takes the form of detention and conviction on 'merely' criminal charges, which supports a public rhetoric of common criminality. Yet accusations of political foul play are constant concomitants, providing a continual reminder of the state's purported provision of adequate channels for any opposition.

The political crime model is to all appearances at a considerable intellectual remove from the unjust war model. Despite persistent criticism of terrorist attacks as indiscriminate and cowardly, the state is, as we have seen, unwilling to regard them as *war* crimes, rather than as solely crimes against domestic law. Yet the political crime model may have difficulty in specifying what the political ends of the terrorist are without invoking the notion of war which it seeks to avoid; for the political motives of the terrorist seem to be precisely those required for war – to deprive a government of control over some or all of its territories, usually because the state's legitimacy there is under challenge. Nor is it clear how the terrorists might hope to achieve this objective – short of a negotiated settlement – without a war or insurrection, once they have the capacity or the support for it. A state under terrorist attack recognises this. It is always ready to move from a constabulary response to a military one should the occasion demand it.

This is presupposed in the presentation of the terrorist's victim as *innocent*. Only in very unusual circumstances (perhaps where a killer has taken the law into his own hands, for example) might outrage at an ordinary murder be expressed in terms of declarations of the victim's innocence. Yet it is not just civilian victims, but policemen and even soldiers or politicians who are so described when they fall prey to terrorist attacks. The point here is not of course that they are *not* innocent: it is that describing them as innocent *or* not innocent presupposes a warlike motive on the part of their attackers, for it employs the condition for a permissible attack under just war theory. The innocence claimed for the terrorist's targets underlines the fact that they, unlike the terrorist, are following out the 'accepted codes of behaviour' within a legitimate political system. Were they politicians or soldiers within another type of system without such codes they would be potentially legitimate targets for attack. The denial of belligerent status to terrorists in liberal democracies thus underscores rather than denies their warlike aims. Furthermore it reveals that recognition of the existence of internal war lies wholly within the prerogative of the state.

Under the political crime model terrorism is not to be thought of as indiscriminate killing in circumstances where discrimination is possible and approved. The codes of behaviour the terrorist breaches are in this sense unlike both codes for conduct in war and what has been described as the *political* code of anti-state violence.[11] Under this code, apparently adhered to by nineteenth-century revolutionaries, it is the agents and politicians of supposedly oppressive states who are to be targeted, not the ordinary citizens who are the victims of their oppression.

But while that may be an acceptable code in actually oppressive states, the political crime model presupposes that it is inapplicable to liberal democracies. Here, since no political crimes are deemed justifiable, no code of conduct for political criminals can be necessary. Distinctions in political reaction to attacks on different types of terrorist target are minimised in the public discourse of outrage – although of course any enormities are emphasised, of which direct attacks upon civilians are certainly the most shocking, the publicity for them serving to disguise the precise political targeting in others.

POLITICAL CRIME

The political crime model of terrorism, as I have presented it, presupposes that in the kind of liberal democratic state to which it applies not only is terrorism unjustified but so is *all* politically motivated crime. It is worth pausing to investigate various types of political crime and the circumstances in which they may be justified. (The categories which I shall be employing here have no positivist underpinnings.)

We can regard political crimes as crimes committed for any political end or as the expression of any political belief, where the perpetrator is acting as a member of a political group or supporter of a political cause rather than merely as a private individual. The latter distinction is an important one, though elusive to capture except by way of examples. The freelance operator who robs a bank to boost party funds is not committing a political crime in the way a member of an IRA cell doing this would be. Nor is the person who poisons meat-based food products in the secret hope of furthering animal rights, unlike the one who publicly announces this as their aim. Openness is not, of course, of the essence in these cases; but a certain notion of acting in a public way is, and the notions of public act and public role are intimately, though complicatedly, related. This notion is most notably exemplified in terrorist claims of responsibility for the acts of violence which they commit.

We can begin a rough categorisation of political crimes by distinguishing those of which the point is to overthrow the existing constitutional structures of the state from those of which it is not. The former include not only secessionist insurgency and the like, but also violent revolution which seeks to replace a bourgeois constitution by a workers' state or vice versa. Apart from such apparently *treasonable* acts, campaigns of law-breaking to change the suffrage or even to secure constitutional amendments for or against abortion ought to be included here. They too seek to change the nature of the state by fundamental modifications in either its government or membership. We may term these acts of *anti-state disobedience*, while by contrast *civil disobedience* overtly aims only to make changes within the existing constitutional structures of the state, to secure nuclear disarmament, for example, or improved animal rights.[12]

A second distinction transects the first, namely that between coercive and non-coercive disobedience. The former aims to exert pressure which, if strong enough, would force through the desired changes. But what counts as coercion? This is a difficult question which cannot detain us here.[13] I shall regard coercion for our purposes as limiting other's choices through actions that fall outside a normal pattern of mutual relationships. This is very vague but it does do some necessary work. It prevents us describing the businesslike bank manager who threatens to bounce my cheques as coercing me into making a deposit, while allowing us to say that the unbusinesslike one who threatens to reveal my gambling debts to my wife does just that. Whether we say that strikers are *forcing* their employer to increase his pay offer will depend not on whether what they do is unfair, but on whether we regard such industrial action as outside the normal pattern of mutual relationships between employees and their employer. We would, if we regarded that relationship as determined by their contract of employment, though arguably this is to take too narrow a view of it. A mutual relationship, then, is one in which the ways in which each may limit the choices of the other are accepted and, broadly speaking, agreed. The conception of coercion employed is roughly that of a limitation of choice other than in a relationship in which I have chosen to accept the possibility of such a limitation. This raises very difficult questions about what relationships I have chosen or agreed to, rather than ones I find myself in or, theoretically worse, am forced into. Agreement, however, must mean something: a relationship is not mutually agreed if it would be imposed willy nilly. So soldiers can be forced to retreat by an enemy advance even though this is part of their normal pattern of relationships with the enemy. That relationship is not, at least in these matters (in contrast to others that concern the care of prisoners and so forth) a *mutual* one. Sketchy as it is, the present conception will do the necessary classificatory work for my present purposes.

Political disobedience can, third, be sub-divided into violent and non-violent. The former comprises acts of physical violence or the threat of such acts, or acts or the threat of them which have consequences foreseeably similar to those of acts or threats of physical violence themselves. Non-violent disobedience will comprise a whole galaxy of acts or threats of them from general strikes to non-payment of Poll Taxes. Clearly violence will normally be coercive. But the possibility of symbolic violence being employed for merely expressive purposes should not be discounted.[14] Punitive acts are often of this sort, since if the risk of being subjected to them is small they would have little or no tendency to constrain the class of people threatened with them. They may however come to make them see their own behaviour differently. Or at least that may be their intention.

Finally one should make a distinction between cases where the breaking of a law is inessential to the point of the act, and cases where disobedience is essential to it. That a terrorist attack is murder under the law is largely incidental to the terrorist's intentions in making it. Coercive acts will normally be of this first sort, though not necessarily so. A really concerted campaign of law-breaking may be intended to force a change in the law through making it inoperable. Many, though not all, acts of civil disobedience are intended, not usually through coercion, to change the very law they break.[15] Others are intended to effect some change in policy by showing that ordinarily law-abiding citizens are prepared on this issue to break the law – *which* law gets broken is commonly determined by the publicity which breaking it attracts, or by its association with the policy objected to. The act of disobedience is a symbolic one. In all these cases disobedience is essential to the act.

A great range of political crimes is possible. Each may be justified in different circumstances. The *mildest* type of case – and that which finds most defenders – is that of civil disobedience that is non-coercive, non-violent but essentially unlawful. This, unlike inessentially unlawful disobedience cannot be viewed as *disregard* for law, but makes its point by way of a dramatic protest that harms no one and seeks only to change their lives, not to constrain their choices. It is, it may be suggested, justified when other attempts at getting a case heard have been unsuccessful, even in a democratic state where a settled consensus can drown out minority voices.

The general principle behind this justification is that there may be grievances which cannot be adequately aired within existing constitutional structures, but that, once aired, can be fairly attended to within the structures. No one, it is implied, should have a grievance that cannot be aired; it is an article of faith that the liberal democratic state can deal with them. But suppose that it does not: why should the licence to commit certain political crimes in order to persuade the state to deal with grievances not extend to committing these crimes to change the state itself? For surely it is implausible to claim that liberal democracies always do, or even can, handle the grievances of minorities fairly. In particular, as we shall see, they cannot adequately deal with the grievances of minorities who wish to protect their own persistently neglected interests.

In such cases it would be idle to suppose that non-coercive disobedience would be effective. The majority is not prepared to be persuaded. And if coercive disobedience is required it may be that only violence would exert the necessary pressure. Violent crimes are likely to exemplify inessentially unlawful disobedience, although if the authority of the state is being challenged, they may again become essentially unlawful – expressing defiance of the most basic laws for protecting the rights of citizens and thereby putting them in fear if they continue to live under the state unchanged. We arrive, then, at the kind of case liberal democratic theorists would refuse to condone – coercive, violent, anti-state disobedience as exemplified in political assassination, riot or terrorism.

TERRORISM AND THE MODERN STATE

The political crime model regards terrorism as an aberrant phenomenon within the modern liberal democratic state. Undoubtedly terrorism is a more limited and a more modern phenomenon than the unjust war model may suggest. The rapacious campaigns of violence waged by robber barons in the Middle Ages were paradigms of the unjust wars that theological doctrines of *jus ad bellum* and *jus in bello* were intended to proscribe. But they do not count as terrorism. The reason is, I suggest, precisely that such campaigns were, in the Middle Ages, treated as *wars* and not simply as crimes. The medieval state with its complex hierarchy of allegiances was unable to claim a monopoly of the use of force. Indeed such military force as it had derived largely from those who, though owing fealty, might levy war against it. Action against them necessarily had the character of internal war. Lacking the apparatus of a police force which expresses the modern state's claim to a monopoly of the use of force in administering the law, the medieval state was in no position to adopt an alternative strategy. These limitations sprang from the nature of the medieval state itself, in contrast to the modern one. Terrorism requires the background of a modern state to be recognisable as a distinctive phenomenon.

In particular it is only within the modern state with its dual responsibilities for preserving national security and civil order that terrorism can arise. Both responsibilities are necessary for violent attacks to count as terrorism. On the one hand the modern state assumes sole responsibility for guarding its inhabitants against attack. Principally such attacks will come from without, in the course of invasions to support territorial claims or whatever. But equally, and sometimes for exactly the same reasons, they may come from within, as in the course of secessionist uprisings. It is because of the state's claim to responsibility for the security of its own citizens that people become anxious that their *own* state should control the territory where they live and thereby preserve their security, rather than some state in which they repose no trust or allegiance. It is unsurprising then that in a system of such states wars of national reunification and of secession, in particular, should be endemic. But evidently on the basis of the state's responsibility for security alone we cannot construct a concept of terrorism by contrast with other forms of insurgency to which the state responds as it would respond to aggression from without. More is required.

What is required is something to explain the *criminal* character of terrorism. This too is rooted in the nature of the modern state. It is not only security that the state is responsible for preserving but civil order. Indeed these dual responsibilities do not, as is commonly supposed,[16] reflect the fact that threats to the safety and wellbeing of citizens can be external or internal. Threats to security may clearly be either, but the way in which the state protects its citizens is just by preserving civil order within its territory. Its defence of its national security is the maintenance of control over the territory within which it can preserve civil order. An internal threat to security will, at least in its early stages, also present itself as a threat to civil order. Terrorists, even though they intend war, cannot wage it without breaking the law by committing murder, criminal damage and so forth. It is the responsibility of the state in maintaining civil order to bring those who are guilty of these acts to justice. It is from the fulfilment of this responsibility by the state that the criminal character of terrorism derives.

In forms of social organisation other than the modern state violent acts can have the character of both war and crime. But only if war is waged against the body responsible both for preserving security and for enforcing the law, by reference to which the warlike acts are criminal, will those acts be terrorist. It is reported[17] that among the Nuer people there are, or used to be, warlike attacks over grazing rights which involved crimes against fellow tribesmen. Yet these do not constitute terrorism as there is no central political organisation in the tribe responsible for preserving security within its lands against such attacks. The wars that occur thus have the character of external conflicts between *separate* political entities with distinct, though sometimes contentious, territorial claims. The absence of a central political organisation with security functions does not however prevent actions within these wars from being treated as crimes by reference to common laws and customs. In this respect a *single* political entity constituted by the whole tribe is involved, and a single authority is accepted and respected even if it lacks the power to *enforce* its judgements. The warriors can see themselves, as the tribal authorities see them, as engaging in both war and crime. Terrorism within the modern state cannot, I shall argue, be seen simultaneously as war and crime by those involved with it.

The double character of terrorism as war and crime arises, as I have argued, from the dual responsibilities of the modern state. When the state confronts enemies from outside or criminals who do not threaten war within, the state can exercise these responsibilities without a conflict of responsibility. But when it confronts domestic terrorism it faces such a conflict. If the state confines itself to legal process it risks its own security. If it resorts to military force it acts outside the rule of law it has a duty to uphold: *inter arma leges silent* (amid weapons of war the laws are silent) as the legal tag has it. The terrorist at one and the same time invites both responses, threatening the state's fulfilment of its dual responsibilities.

The natural reaction to this situation is to deny that terrorism can be both war and crime. The state, on the one hand, may assert that terrorism is simply crime and try to deal with it as such. Terrorists, on the other hand, may assert that they are freedom fighters and deny that their actions are crimes. Yet they are usually in no position to offer an alternative source of authority for the maintenance of order in the areas in which they operate.

Both attitudes express not judgements as to the facts, but decisions on how to act in the light of the facts. For whereas terrorism can be both war and crime, it cannot simultaneously be treated as such, on either side. The state cannot simultaneously operate both the civil law and the rules of war against terrorists. It has to choose which to apply. If it is to regard its opponents as terrorists it has to operate the law against them. Terrorists, for their part, cannot sustain their political role *and* admit that they are criminals. While if they are to be taken to be waging war they must at least make some pretence of conforming to its rules.

The justification for war, and for the methods employed in war, are *not*, in the system of modern states, those of just war theory, except insofar as just war theory is incorporated into the international law of war or, very differently, deliberately adopted as one of the determinants of policy by a particular state. In the former case just war theory serves to characterise the rules of war and warmaking along positivist lines: it helps to shape the rules which states place themselves under, or under which they are placed in virtue of the power and pressure of the international system, which in its turn reflects those rules to which states in general are prepared to accede. The ultimate authority of these rules is derived, then, from the state, not from some superior authority, such as the Church or natural law. Positivism thus accurately reflects the modern state's claim to *sovereignty* with respect to the rules which bind it. But what determines its acceptance of those rules?

The adoption of rules for war and war-making is judged, in the long run anyway, to be in the interests of the state. The particular rules adopted reflect that judgement. When a state embarks on war, it does so because it believes that constraining itself by these rules advances its policy interests. The positivist doctrine of what war consists in is mirrored by Clausewitz's famous description, 'war is the continuation of politics by other means':[18] the states that determine for reasons of policy what war should be like embark upon it in the pursuit of policy objectives. This implies that it would be irrational for a state to fight a war that was not limited by its political goals. Among these will very likely be the maintenance of the sympathy and support of its own citizens and actual or potential allies, thus alienating them from the enemy. In those circumstances the adoption of an approach infused by just war thinking may be politically astute. But it is only an example of the doctrine that war should be limited by political objectives – it is not essentially a matter of moral judgement.

No doubt it could be argued that terrorists too – investing themselves already with the dignity of the state that they may hope to found – employ just war principles, at least rhetorically, for the same reasons. What is clear is that there is normally nothing the terrorist can do to *force* a state to recognise that a war is under way so long as its political goals can be served by means other than war. If its political goals really are confined to the maintenance of civil order for part of its territory – that is to say if the terrorists are not perceived as a threat to national *security* – then it is highly unlikely that a military response can be elicited.

These considerations are quite general. They apply to all states of the modern type, of which not all contemporary states may be examples, not just to those with political democratic underpinnings to their claims of sovereignty. The responsibility for civil order and the consequent tendency to treat small-scale insurgency as crime, and therefore terrorism, applies to all modern states. There is no reason, contrary to the political crime view, to think of terrorism as confined to liberal democracies. It is possible in any modern state. Its criminal character has nothing to do with whether it is justified or not. It simply reflects the best option available to the state in pursuing its policy objectives. Here questions of fairness to opponents and so forth have no place – or rather they have a place only indirectly to the extent to which the state may need, in pursuit of its policy, to justify its methods with respect to broader goals. For it must not be forgotten that the modern state pursues and must pursue its own interests: it is not, for all its pretensions to the contrary, a disinterested instrument of justice.

Chapter 5

Community and conflict

UNJUST WAR AND THE COMMUNITY

Our reactions to terrorism, as to much political violence and insurgency, are shaped, I have suggested, by conflicting influences. On the one hand we react to what commonly though not invariably appears as *injustice* – as adversely affecting people without adequate justification. The kinds of intuition captured by just war theory, themselves drawing on divergent analogies, play an important part in shaping these reactions. On the other hand we react to what often appears as *lawless*; as unconstrained by law or by proper procedure. And here we are influenced by the positivist thinking that underlies the political crime model of terrorism, internalised by us in our role of citizens of a modern state. In the former mode we are prone to listen to justifications, grievances and regrets, to assess their strength, passion and sincerity, to revise our own reactions or to defend them. In the latter we are apt to be intolerant of excuses, resolute in safeguarding what we take for granted as our own rights and interests against the depredations of wrong-doers. It would be an over-simplification to see these as stark alternatives, between which we have to oscillate. But there is, I suggest, a tension which reflects the unsettled state of our view of terrorism. It reflects, I shall argue, a more general stress in our conception of the political community itself.

Given the historical roots of just war theory it is unsurprising that the conception of community associated with the unjust war model of terrorism is in origin a medieval one. On this *communitarian* conception,[1] as I shall term it, the community is regarded as a group living a common life in accordance with its own rules, but which in practice needs a ruler to enforce them when communal pressures are inadequate to the task. The possibility of a common life in accordance with rules however does not derive in principle from the presence of a ruler. It derives from shared values and a common concern to live a life in accordance with them. A ruler rules justly only when she upholds those values and conforms to them. That is why members of the community have a duty to obey her.

The only justification for disobedience and, in extreme cases, for rebellion or tyrannicide derives from the ruler breaking faith with the community and failing in her duty towards it. In this case the community is able to assert its identity independently of its ruler by rising as a body or by giving its authority to others to act on its behalf. In such a situation the community itself is waging war, but this is a quite exceptional case, for in general it is the ruler who wages war, either to protect the community from those who would wrong it, or to defend her own position against rivals from without or from within.

It is the problems of the latter kind of cause for war that permits just war theory its particular emphasis on the immunity of the civilian community in time of war or civil strife. While its members are enjoined to show loyalty to their present ruler so long as she rules without unconscionable injustice, and to defer to her judgement of whether war is needed to protect them, nevertheless it is in general she not they who is a party to the war. By the communitarian conception wars are struggles between potential rulers for the control of the territory that supports communities, and the concern of the community is that it should emerge from such wars as unscathed as possible. And why should it suffer? If it is rulers who wage war then it is they who must bear the burden of responsibility for the justice of their cause and the fairness of their means. The relationship of ruler to ruled is thus exactly reflected in the just war theory doctrine, which forbids deliberate attacks upon the innocent. These doctrines derive from natural or, possibly, divine law. They are not the laws of kings and rulers but laws that kings and rulers as much as their subjects must obey. They prescribe codes of conduct which limit the extent to which rulers can draw civilian communities into their disputes without injustice. They elaborate a concept of the innocent civilian as one whose essence is exhausted by his or her civilian life as a member of a community, depending not at all upon membership of a body organised to defend it.

The Communitarian conception I have elaborated may seem an archaic one, unrepresented in contemporary thinking. Insofar as just war theory is part of modern thought, it may be said that it depends not on such conceptions but on broader moral principles about the scope and limits of war as a way of settling disputes. I do not deny that it might be placed upon other foundations but I doubt whether its old foundations have crumbled entirely away. Whatever the system of government in a state, those that rule have enormous power. Their use of it ostensibly on behalf of the community should, we often think, involve the community as little as possible. In particular the risks of vainglorious, imprudent or self-interested uses of power must not rebound upon the community more than can be helped. Were the community to be consulted on the terms under which it should be ruled it would insist upon these conditions. Thus to rule on any other terms is to take advantage of the powers that ruling brings. Such thoughts as these, I suggest, still weigh heavily in our unreflective sentiments about the relation of citizens to state and create a degree of detachment between the two.

It is this detachment which enables attacks upon the state from within to be, to some extent, the subject of impersonal moral scrutiny. Current rulers may have an inadequate title to the territory they control. Or they may, at least in some part of it, govern unjustly and contrary to the good of the community there. But it is as well to be sceptical too of those who challenge rulers and of those who claim to represent some community in acting against them. They also are aspiring rulers or their surrogates, and as such their motives must also be suspect. Ordinary civilians would do well, except where there is the clearest possible case for acting otherwise, to keep clear of such disputes.

On the communitarian conception the proper recourse for rulers against those who oppose them is war; for it is by war that the power to rule is won or lost. Doubtless rulers will use the law against rebels. But the law belongs essentially to the community, not to its rulers, and the community need have no reason to see rebels, so long as they do not attack civilians, as acting in breach of its laws. Similarly the community need have no reason to regard the state's security forces as entitled to the protection of the law against direct attack, as are civilians. The communitarian conception underpins this feature of the unjust war model of terrorism which, unlike the political crime model, sees attacks on civilians in a quite different light from attacks on the forces of the state. Civil strife is of course a very great evil creating many perils and causing much suffering. It does not, however, *inevitably* destroy the community. That is why the community can, and usually should, detach itself from the war that rages around it.

And this attitude, that internal war is another's war not our own, is surely still a powerful one. It explains the respect we have for those who try to carry on living their ordinary lives in the midst of civil war or of terrorist and counter-terrorist activity.

STATISM AND POLITICAL CRIME

We turn from an image of people like the 'harmless agricultural folk'[2] who are the traditional paradigm of innocence in war, going doggedly about their daily work while insurgency and counter-insurgency explode about them, to a pair of different scenes: on the one hand 'the warre of every man against every man' that Hobbes envisioned; on the other the harnessing of citizens to the efforts of a government to establish order within secure borders. Only through the second, Hobbes would have us believe, is there a hope of the first being avoided. We have seen reason to doubt the inevitability of this contrast; though a determined Hobbesian could respond by pointing to the rapidity with which power relations tend to re-establish themselves as evidence of their necessity to prevent what would in the long term be violent anarchy. Empirical observations are unlikely to resolve the issue, which is rooted in contrary intuitions about the nature of political communities.

The Hobbesian intuition offers us a *statist* conception of political community. The community is a group identified by its subordination to a common government which has the power to enforce laws through being able both to secure obedience to them and to control territory in which to do so. Membership of the community, therefore, has no essential connection with the sharing of values. The same laws are kept by all because disobedience is punished. To apply these laws impartially is to govern justly. This is what prevents the otherwise inevitable disintegration of social bonds through violent conflict. The very existence of the community depends on the continuation of government; its members have an overwhelming interest in maintaining it, particularly in the face of an external threat. They are identified in part through membership of a body, the state, which acts in defence of this interest.

The statist conception of political community is better tailored to the conditions of the modern state than its communitarian rival. It recognises that the maintenance of order is accomplished by the impartial application of its laws even to those seeking to take power by violence, since resort to military force would plunge the commu-

nity into the dreaded 'warre of every man against every man'. Even
if actual disorder might be no greater if opposed by military force, it
would have a different character: it would no longer be *lawless* violence, precisely because the state no longer uses the law against it. It
would, instead, be simply a struggle for power. But the state has a
duty to the community to enforce the law so long as this is possible.
As soon as it does not it is no longer treating those who defy it as
members of the community, but rather as it would treat external enemies. And that is to concede that it no longer has power across what
has been regarded as the whole community. Its claim to be obeyed in
return for the security it offers is correspondingly weakened.

We find in the statist conception the underpinnings of the political
crime model of terrorism. Its refusal to treat attacks upon the agents
of the state – be they military or civil – any differently from attacks
upon ordinary civilians is easily explained. All are accorded the protection of the law within the territory of the state and attacks on any
are to be treated similarly. Only when the state is *unable* to do this, for
example when invaded by an external aggressor, is a different mode
of response appropriate. For that is war. So we see in the political
crime model's refusal to regard terrorists as waging war a reflection of
the state's determination to resort to war only *in extremis*.

War, in Hobbes's view, is the state of nature which *always* prevails
between established states.[3] Like men, states have interests that could
often be furthered by attacks on others. Yet there is nothing by way
of a superior power to regulate relations between them. Customs
there may be, but with no body adequate to enforce them they will
in the long term be defied by states who seek to pursue their own
interests by exploiting their more powerful position. At any given
time the 'war' between states is likely to involve no more than a
defensive posture against possible attack – the maintenance of
armies and weaponry and the collection of intelligence. It is this that
deters attack: there is no other power to prevent it. But whereas
Hobbes thinks of civil war as incompatible with continuing social
and economic life it is precisely the possibility of this that is secured
by external war. Hobbes has no doubt that it can continue, because,
despite war with an external enemy, internal bonds need not be
weakened. It is these, he thinks, that must collapse in civil strife as a
result of the impotence of a single common authority to sustain
them.

What happens in internal conflicts cannot be passed of as simply
a dispute over who should exercise power; for the government is the

community's government in the strongest possible sense – without it the community would not exist. So attacks on it are attacks upon the community. But, at least where such attacks are widespread, we shall no longer be able to identify a single community as being attacked: we can only identify some of its members as open to attack by others. And that is the war of all against all. Nor can we easily identify *separate* communities struggling for territory here. Sometimes such a description is inappropriate anyway, as in revolutionary war. But even where it is appropriate, on a statist conception it is applicable only when each side already has a common authority to make good the breakdown of the old order, and then it becomes an external war.

I have already conceded that Hobbesian apprehensions as to the breakdown of the community in civil strife are very strong. They evince the power of the statist conception in ordinary thought. We do frequently think of our orderly relations with others as mediated by mutual acknowledgement of the same political authority. We are nervous when others decline to make such acknowledgement. Conversely the feeling that nothing is owed to the state can present itself as a licence for riot and disorder: an inverted recognition of the kind of relationship between citizens that the modern state – anxious to defend its powers as indispensable – assiduously seeks to foster.

For Hobbes the existence of *any* state, however authoritarian, is to the advantage of its citizens: to rebel against it is senselessly rash. The political crime model, as I have presented it, makes a different assumption. It is that liberal democratic states, and they alone, are safe from reasonable rebellion. Conclusive arguments against violent opposition are available only in a democratic state that can fairly consider the claims of different interest groups. Any other kind of state is potentially unstable and lacks the degree of social cohesion that adherence to democratically agreed rules can provide. A democratic state is the political property of its citizens, so that an attack on it is an attack which threatens them as a body.

Hobbes himself supposed that the authority of the state derives from popular consent to it. Yet it is hard to see how the existence of such consent could be established, most especially in a state which has, as Hobbes thought it should have, the power to *compel* obedience. In a democratic state, however, the consent of the citizens can be demonstrated, it may be argued, from the fact that they themselves determine its government. Having agreed to it they have a duty to obey it. That is the force of the political crime model's emphasis on the breach by terrorists of proper procedures. They are not playing the political game.

We have seen why any government, on the statist conception, must so far as it is able, treat acts of terrorism as crimes. But arguably only liberal democratic governments are entitled to go on to condemn them for breaching the rules, adherence to which makes the state the citizens' own. Not that this weighs heavily with terrorists, who deny the state that entitlement. Yet it serves, in a way that the mere punishment of terrorism does not, to dramatise the attacks of terrorists as attacks upon the community itself, as represented by its properly elected government. Since in a liberal democracy the government can plausibly be viewed as merely the representative of the community, attacks on it can be presented as aimed at the community. The terrorist by contrast must seek to undermine these links and, in particular, to offer an alternative view of how a state or states might belong to this community or to these communities. He is obliged to deny the entitlement of the established state to be the proper political organisation for his community.

One way, and, I would suggest, an extremely common way in which this may be achieved is to seek to undermine the statist conception of community itself. It would be very natural were the terrorist to do so, since statism identifies communities principally in terms of established states, and it is established states that terrorists characteristically challenge. Sometimes of course terrorists may already regard themselves as members of some proto-state ready to step into the breach when the existing state collapses under pressure. But this is rare except among large-scale guerrilla movements which seek to impose their rule on areas over which they may have a measure of military control. What is more usual is for terrorists to claim to support already existing communities although these lack any form of government other than the state under attack. This claim presupposes a communitarian rather than a statist conception of political community.

The communitarian model better fits, as we have seen, the terrorist's demand to be treated as a soldier and not a criminal. It supports a possible claim by him to be ridding the community of a tyrant. And, of course, it consorts naturally with secessionist campaigns to establish separate states for what are thought of as pre-existing communities. In many cases, then, the clash of terrorist and state is not just a conflict as to what political organisation there should be for people in a territory, but a conflict over what the relations between peoples and their political organisations are. Underlying violent struggles there lurk philosophical arguments.

COLLECTIVE RESPONSIBILITY

The political crime model of terrorism and its associated statist conception of the political community appear to carry with them a chilling consequence for ordinary citizens. Since it is the citizens as a whole, rather than their rulers, who constitute the entity which may be party to a conflict, namely the state, it is they who seem to be the natural and perhaps legitimate targets of terrorists who wage a campaign against it. We may be led to the view that the citizen body is collectively responsible for any injustice the terrorist seeks to rectify and that, in consequence, attacks upon its members may be justified.[4] If that was so the apparent indiscriminateness of much terrorist killing would be explained and, furthermore, exonerated.

This line of argument, however, is over simple. Though the notion of collective responsibility may play a part in the message that the terrorist campaign aims to convey, it seldom plays the part suggested by statism of justifying the terrorists' choice of victim. The impression that it does so justify their choice is, instead, one that the leaders of modern states have no wish to dispel, since it may appear to legitimise their own actions and to discharge them from any special responsibility.

To start with, it is evident that it is only if terrorists think of their killings as revolutionary justice, or some other kind of punitive measure, that they can be aimed at ordinary citizens as sharing equally in the guilt accruing from the injustices of the state. This is only one type of terrorist killing and a comparatively unusual one, typified by assassination. Assassination is not in itself a form of war, though it may constitute an objective in a war intended to punish injustice. When such a war is launched the intended victim is likely to be protected by troops who must themselves be attacked whether they share in his guilt or not. It is because terrorists principally think of themselves as engaged in war and attacking such targets that their killings do not usually have the character of assassination.

When terrorists do embark upon a campaign of assassination it will typically be aimed at those who bring about or benefit from the injustices of the state. Internal terrorists must deny *general* collective responsibility or they themselves, as citizens of the state, would share in it and constitute targets as legitimate as any others! We can im-

agine – perhaps there have been – political suicides by ordinary citizens to atone for collective guilt and bring it to the attention of
others. One can scarcely imagine them coupled with a terrorist campaign; for the terrorist believes that in actively opposing injustice he
escapes any share of responsibility for it.

This is not to say that terrorists do not hold groups *within* the state
collectively responsible for its injustices. This can sometimes give rise
to sectarian or ethnic violence. But it is doubtful whether in these
cases the motive is normally *punishment* of any sort. Rather terrorist
killings are likely to be aimed at deterring other members of the
group from engaging in the alleged injustice, or in some cases simply
at intimidating them. At the best such actions might be described as
defensive. No responsibility on their part is required, however, for people who constitute a potential threat to become legitimate targets
when self-defence is at issue.

Indeed to defend oneself against a state which is oppressive may,
arguably, require attacks upon its members even though they bear no
guilt for the state's injustices. There are of course many cases here. At
one extreme lie those where guilt can be pinned upon some individuals – a ruthless tyrant and his henchmen perhaps – who themselves
terrorise others into performing acts which are unjust and recognised
to be unjust by those who reluctantly and fearfully perform them.
There is no need to employ any notion of collective responsibility
here to justify attacks upon the tyrant's lackeys. What justifies it is
simply that they are instrumental in performing unjust acts of the
sort that have to be resisted.

The same applies to cases at the other extreme, where collective
responsibility for some activity can be attributed to a group whose
members are equally implicated but who are quite unaware that
what they do constitutes an injustice to others. An example might be
white settlers who innocently think of the indigenous inhabitants
whose livelihoods they threaten as simply savages. Although perhaps
individually blameless they may all equally be legitimate targets in an
anti-colonial terrorist campaign. It is, one might say, the colonial *system* that needs to be smashed.[5] But it can only be smashed by
attacking those who operate it, even though those who operate it are
themselves shaped by it in their own attitudes and judgements.

The result may itself seem cruelly unjust, for blameless individuals
are greatly harmed. Yet the *system* is not blameless. It perpetrates
injustice, not just suffering. And it does so in a way that can be
explained by its working to the benefit of those who operate it, as ef-

ficiently as if it were planned to do so. If it were planned to do so we could not fail to impute knowledge of its injustices to its planners. Such knowledge cannot be attributed to the system, unplanned as we suppose it is. Yet this should not prevent us from regarding it as blameworthy. In particular we shall seek to bring those who operate it to see how it works and to make such moral judgements of it. That they did not do so previously, however, is not necessarily to be regarded as a moral fault in them: it may be simple ignorance. So it is not apposite to attempt to distribute blame for the wrongs of the system among its operators on the grounds that there were things they could or should have done to stop it. That may just not be true.

We need, then, to distinguish sharply between collective responsibility which is *distributive*, in the sense that it implies individual responsibility among the members, from that which is *non-distributive* in the sense that it implies no individual responsibility on the part of members in general.[6] The former is exemplified by an English town council, whose members share in the responsibility for the consequences of its decisions; the latter is examplified by the town itself, whose citizens do not bear individual responsibility for what is done in its name, as this is decided by its council. The statist view suggests that the members of a political community each bear responsibility for the actions of the state which constitutes it, since, first, no distinction can be drawn between the community and its political organisation, the state, and second, the members are taken to have, at least tentatively, agreed to this form of organisation.

The last point is a crucial one. On the statist conception, the community is not simply constituted by its political organisation as a body of serfs might be constituted by a common villeinage. The government of the state is taken to have an authority which derives from popular consent.[7] The state is thereby taken to be an *association*[8] – a body of people formed for a definite purpose, in this case, security, and organised to achieve that end. It is characteristic of associations, though not perhaps invariably so, that their members share in the collective responsibility of the association for its acts. This derives from the fact that they are thought of as accepting such a responsibility in agreeing to membership.

It is the associational character of the state that generates distributive collective responsibility if anything does, not the fact, if it is a fact, that the state has democratic decision-making procedures.[9] Participation in these is at most evidence of consent to the association. It is for this reason that it might be right to hold even members of a political minority responsible for the majority's decision, since they might be taken to have accepted that decision through political participation. Yet, on reflection, it is by no means clear that such participation does *prove* acceptance of or consent to a political association.

In the first place, registering eligibility to vote or even voting itself are, in many democracies, required of citizens by law. In these cases anyway participation cannot be viewed as acceptance of the system, since no rejection of it is permitted. Even where rejection is permitted, mere participation in a process to which one is offered no alternative but exclusion from *any* political influence can scarcely demonstrate acceptance of it: I may for example object strongly to the way in which, in a workplace ballot, a question is posed in such a way as to split opposition to the employer's proposals; but I may nonetheless participate in an effort to reject them. Furthermore, as this example shows, democratic procedures may be adopted by institutions where there is no question of an *association* being created by them: it may simply be convenient to have people on one's side, especially if one can control their voting behaviour. Voting along with others does not demonstrate consent to associate with them, even if others think of themselves as forming such an association (e.g. of local residents). In the absence of formal procedures for taking up or laying down membership there is indeed nothing which can conclusively demonstrate such consent.

The upshot of this discussion is to cast doubt on the view that the situation of citizens in the modern state is such as to generate a convincing argument for holding them individually responsible for its acts. There is little force in the claim that simply in virtue of their citizenship they may be legitimate targets for punitive action by terrorists on behalf of groups subjected to injustice. Yet if the state is, as I have implied is possible, itself blameworthy, who *may* be punished for its acts? In the absence, let us implausibly suppose, of individual responsibility for particular injustices, it is hard to see how anyone could count as being *punished* for its acts. And yet the state itself might be punished through sanctions against its agents. The holding of office in an unjust state may render someone liable even though as an individual he or she has no responsibility for its injustices; for the state is an organisation which acts through human agents, and these must bear some liability for its acts, in proportion to the degree to which they are instrumental in acting on its behalf. It is not usually possible, therefore, for the government of a democratic state to disclaim liability by asserting that it was only carrying out the will of the people. This will be a plausible defence only where a majority of the people can be attributed individual responsibility for the consequences of their unjust will; and even then their agents in government must share in their responsibility. In the conditions of the modern state this case will surely be a rare one.

To escape this kind of conclusion it is sometimes claimed that the ordinary citizen is morally blameworthy for the injustices of his or her state, not by acts of participation but rather by omissions – by failing, for example, to oppose its injustices or by making no attempt to rectify them.[10] No doubt such omissions are often blameworthy, in particular where they serve the interests of those who are guilty of them and are recognised as doing so. Then there seems little moral difference between, for example, doing nothing to relieve hunger amongst some group within the state and acting self-interestedly in a way that causes hunger. It is in such cases that collective responsibility may be attributed to the dominant group and distributed as individual moral responsibility at least among those who do by their individual acts of omission bring about the injustice.

One way to view both kinds of case is as breaches of duty. Within a single political community there are, we may suppose, duties owed to each other by the constituent groups, breaches of which give those who are wronged cause for resentment and indignation which may issue in punitive acts against those partly to blame. Yet the conception of the community operating here is scarcely the statist one, even as supplemented by liberal democracy. For on that conception there are no duties within the community prior to those imposed by the state; and in liberal democratic theory these will be determined simply by majority voting. The notion that there are duties that hold in virtue of the character of the political community itself presupposes instead some version of the communitarian conception, so that collective responsibilities flow from what the community as a whole owes to its parts. The breaches of duty for which a dominant group are guilty in acting unjustly towards another derive from their failure to play their proper part as members of the community, frustrating the community as a whole from carrying out these responsibilities.

We see, then, that it is from a communitarian rather than from a statist conception that terrorists are likely to act if they present themselves as engaging in revolutionary justice against a dominant group. There are evidently two forms which this may take. One accepts that there is a single community within which duties have been breached, so that sanctions are required to recall those responsible to their duty – although because of their politically dominant position these cannot be imposed through the community's ordinary political structures. Marxist terrorism can sometimes be seen in this light. Another form of revolutionary justice, however, views the persistent breach of duty as indicative of the lack of any single community: it sees the dominant group as self-interestedly exploiting a separate community. It is not a breach of *intra*-communal duty which is then to be punished but rather the violation of a community's rights; and this gives rise to a typical case of terrorism in support of independence movements.

The scope for justification in such cases is limited if they involve punitive attacks on ordinary citizens held to share in collective responsibility. In many instances, as I have indicated, it is rather the 'system' that is to blame and then attacks on it have a different character. But even where groups of ordinary citizens can be held responsible their own individual share in guilt will commonly be small. They benefit relatively little and no doubt with an eye to their own advantage rather than to the disadvantage of others. This is especially true where acts of omission are involved. It is all too easy to avert one's eyes from the consequences for others of simply going on with one's own life without making changes that might improve their situation. Viewed as *punishment* for such neglect murderous attacks would be wholly disproportionate. Viewed as acts of exemplary deterrence they will seem arbitrary and unfair. No justification for them is to be found along these lines. But that is not to say that, as the actions of desperate and disadvantaged people, they are not intelligible.

TERRORISM AND MODERNITY

I have argued that a good deal of anti-state terrorism reflects an attachment to older communitarian ways of thinking, rather than to contemporary statism. What makes terrorism a *modern* phenomenon, not encountered until the modern state comes into being, is the conflict between old and new conceptions which makes it possible, and which is expressed in its dual character as war and crime. Yet in arguing for this view I fly in the face of another and perhaps more immediately attractive one; that far from representing an older way of thinking, terrorism carries modern assumptions to their ultimate and unacceptable conclusion.[11] This view sees terrorism as a form of modernism in two distinct respects: first, it sees it as a struggle on behalf of the 'people' which reflects modern doctrines of popular sovereignty and self-determination; second, it sees it as utilitarian, substituting for more traditional ethical prohibitions the modern view of ends as justifying means. I shall take these points in order.

It is democratic statism, as I have presented it, that arises natural-ly from doctrines of popular sovereignty and self-determination. Popular sovereignty accords citizens an equal share in the political power of the state. It is not actually implied by the view that the state gains its authority through popular consent – since this is consistent with sovereignty resting in the hands of a ruler rather than the peo-ple – but it does naturally go along with it. What is more, if the people are to control the power they exercise then democracy is a natural corollary of popular sovereignty. The principle of self-deter-mination follows from basing the state's authority on consent; for this permits the people, by giving or withholding consent, to determine what their state will be and how it will be organised. Putting these ideas together yields a general conception of the people as the source of legitimate political power, and the people's will as the determinant of how political power should be organised and exercised – a con-ception which is exemplified in democratic statism.

It is true that a great many terrorist campaigns claim to act on behalf of 'the people' who are thought of as denied their political rights by others.[12] An obvious example is Marxist terrorism which sees the people in terms of a working-class majority denied its right to a major share of political power by a dominant bourgeoisie. Another example is nationalist terrorism of the sort which allows that a section of the population has a fair share in existing political struc-tures but claims for them the right to a separate political structure in which they are dominant. Such cases are clearly compatible with the statist conception, and it would be quite wrong to deny that this con-ception is absent from terrorist ideology. Since a part of the point of ideology is to *persuade*, it is likely to utilise ideas in common currency at the time, as those of statism are. To talk of acting on behalf of the people or of expressing the will of the people has rhetorical force in campaigns against the state precisely because it is the kind of talk the state itself employs to justify its own position and actions. But the similarity should not mislead us. Although many terrorist campaigns do claim to be part of the people's struggle, their notion of 'the peo-ple' should not be assumed to be the same as that of statism.

Judged by the criteria of liberal democracy the terrorist's claim of acting on behalf of the people or of expressing their will often sounds hollow. Seldom do terrorists make any attempt to establish the legitimacy of their campaign through conducting referenda for example. Where they put up candidates in elections these commonly gain few votes, even in areas where they allege popular support. Can they really believe that the claims they make of acting on behalf of the people have any democratic justification? Sometimes terrorist groups reply to this line of attack by noting the control that dominant groups within the state can exercise over democratic processes, and even over the attitudes of citizens, which prevent them from adequately expressing or even realising their 'true' interests and attitudes. Sometimes these responses may be justified. Often they are unconvincing to a degree which should raise doubts as to whether statist and liberal democratic ideas are being employed with a more than merely rhetorical point.

The terrorist's deeper answer to liberal democratic criticisms is that liberal democratic procedures do not serve to determine the will of the political community which he represents; for insofar as the terrorist represents the people it is, typically, as a pre-existing community that he claims to represent them, not as individuals wishing to be part of a community. So, even if they have this wish, it is not one which should be expected to take precedence in parliamentary elections, say, over other, perhaps more immediate, concerns. The apparent failure of support for the terrorist's political aim may not, therefore, disconcert him. Even in constitutional referenda there may be other considerations weighing in voters' minds which militate against the 'right' outcome.

In each case the key point is that under statism the people are not voting *as* members of a community; they are voting simply as individuals with a variety of interests. But under the communitarian view a clear distinction can be drawn between someone voting as an individual in pursuit of his own interests and voting as a member of the community in pursuit of its interests.[13] This distinction cannot be easily sustained in terms of the statist view that there is no community independent of what is constituted by its political organisation, and that its *raison d'être* is the benefit of individuals, determined in accordance with democratic theory by their own choices. Yet under communitarianism, unless they are voting as members of a community there is no reason to take their vote as indicative of the community's political will. If they are not, then the terrorist's claim to be acting on their community's behalf cannot be controverted by their votes.

Those the terrorist claims to represent are likely to lack the political organisation necessary to express formally their will as a community. Indeed the provision of such an organisation is precisely what the terrorist's campaign often aims to achieve. It is in the sense in which the community as a whole might express its will with respect to its political organisation that the terrorist is likely to believe in self-determination. It is in the sense that, as members of the community, all are equal in sharing the power the community should have to decide its political affairs that he may believe in popular sovereignty. That is why, whether on the left or the right, there is a strong strain of *collectivism* in most terrorist causes, which stands in sharp contrast to the individualism that characterises the modernity exemplified by statism.

We may turn now to the second feature of modernity which the terrorist may be claimed to illustrate in a dramatically excessive way – utilitarianism. Utilitarianism in its simplest form is the doctrine that the measure of the moral rightness of an act is the degree to which it produces a surplus of satisfaction over distress. It is clear that we can imagine circumstances in which the death of an innocent may sometimes produce such a surplus. In that case it will, on unqualified utilitarian principles, be right. It is no use arguing here that the performance of such an act may undermine the rule against killing the innocent with its overall tendency for the good. This is no longer an example of the situation we set ourselves to imagine in which there really *is* a surplus of satisfaction over distress. We tell a story that allows this to be so by allowing exceptions to the rule, so that if in circumstances of the sort that we imagine it is right to kill innocents, then anyone following the modified rule acts for the best. Nor is it any use arguing that the consequences of such acts are never adequately foreseeable. There is no reason to think that we can foresee the consequences of individual acts less well than we can foretell the consequences of adopting certain rules. We may sometimes be better able to predict that the consequences of killing an innocent person would be to the overall good than to tell that sticking to an exceptionalness rule against it would be. This kind of test case for the acceptability of utilitarianism cannot be bilked.

It is true that terrorists often make what appear to be cynical calculations as to the advantages of breaking moral rules, for example against the killing of innocents. Given the high value they place upon the achievement of their overall goals it may seem that these calculations are utilitarian in character. It would be unsurprising if they were. Utilitarian calculations lie at the heart of much modern decision making. Indeed it is a lively issue whether or not utilitarianism in some form does provide the most acceptable criterion of moral rightness. Although probably incapable of defending exceptionless rules it does have the merit of offering a criterion which makes some sense of the rules we do employ. In doing so it frees them from the limitations of the particular cultural context in which they are to be found.

It is precisely this aspect of utilitarianism that makes one doubt whether it is the ethical principle most commonly employed by terrorists when determining their policies. What is striking about these is often the scale of the apparent disproportion between the suffering they are prepared to inflict upon those on the side of 'the enemy' and that which they are willing to accept on their own side. The lives of those on the enemy's side seem, as we may be inclined to observe, to count for little. What is striking is not so much the calculatedness of attacks as their callousness towards enemies. This is manifest in Marxist terror against 'enemies of the people', in nationalist campaigns of violence against other groups and in sectarian killings. The attitude to others that is evinced is in striking contrast to utilitarian assumptions of human equality in claims for consideration. Instead it carries to an extreme the idea that one has *special* obligations to those to whom one is related by the community, as by kinship. Such codes of special obligation are not thought of as requiring justification in terms of their contribution to *general* happiness. Rather they have a place within particular cultural conceptions of how it is good to live within a community

It is perhaps as an example of such special obligations that the prohibition upon the killing of innocents should be regarded. Paradigmatically innocents are women and children – too weak it is assumed, to pose a danger to a community and, indeed, capable of being absorbed into a community other than their own without any risks to it. There are assumptions here deeply embedded in our particular culture – more deeply embedded than is the medieval view of 'agricultural folk' as harmless. Indeed they are assumptions that are highly questionable. To question them would be to bring to the surface features that underlie our conception of the identity and reproduction of political communities. It is, evidently, a deeply paternalist conception, far removed from the officially undifferentiated individualism of modern statism.

Chapter 6

Reasons for violence

PICTURES OF VIOLENCE

Why choose violence as a political weapon? Is this choice ever justified? These questions are both suspiciously general and potentially
misleading. They make it appear as if the choice of political acts
involving violence is always the choice of a certain kind of *tactic* for
securing one's ends, so that one could then use a general formula to
assess whether such a tactic can be defended given the probability of
its achieving its ends and the certainty of the suffering it causes. This
is, for example, the kind of calculation we should have to make in a
utilitarian approach to the question.[1] Certainly some violent acts are
chosen as a tactic, e.g. to force a grievance into the public eye, in the
manner of the 'propaganda by deed' practised by nineteenth-century Russian revolutionaries.[2] But this is not the original choice of
violence as a permissible form of activity: it is the choice of a particular use of violence after such a choice has already been made. In
fact the *actual* violence of the action chosen is not always a part of the
tactic employed: whether a bomb kills people may be irrelevant to its
intended effect – that it *might* have done suffices. But again we may
say that violence has been chosen, and it is the expression of this
choice which serves as a tactic, though the choice itself need not be
tactical. Indeed, there seems little prospect of any *general* answer to
the question why violence is chosen in terms of the terrorist's tactics:
the intended question concerns not the choice of tactics, but a framework within which certain tactics are possible.

Yet is it enough to characterise the violence of terrorists or insurgents as *expressive*[3] because it is not always chosen as a tactic
calculated to achieve their goals, or not calculated to achieve them
without a quite unnecessary amount or risk of suffering? Violence

can be a spontaneous expression of indignation or apprehension; and it need not be done on the spur of the moment to be spontaneous, in the sense of arising naturally from such a passion; anger or fear can smoulder long before they are expressed. We may well suppose that political violence sometimes has this character, that it is done in a spirit of cold anger or concentrated fear, and that to do it is to follow the urgings of these passions, to achieve the kind of satisfaction, however temporary, that giving appropriate expression to them provides. But equally, political violence may not be in this sense spontaneous. The 'passionate intensity' of the conviction that underlies it may not disturb the professionalism of its agents. The natural association with passion can set up a merely conventional association. Just as a kiss may be a spontaneous expression of affection, it can be a conventional one too, an indication of affection even when affection seeks no expression. Expression is now ritualised: it communicates not as a natural but as a conventional sign, not 'pressed out' of one, but used for a purpose. We are back now to tactics, and to the use of violence chosen, in this case, to make a point about the passions which those it is directed against arouse.

The analogy between political violence and spontaneous violence is a natural but not an inevitable one. It is a way of looking at the situation in which one is placed that shapes, rather than is shaped by, one's feelings about it. It typically involves seeing oneself as the victim of actual or threatened injustice, or as the defender of those who are. It also involves seeing oneself as unprotected in the face of injustice, or as having only one's own resources to rely upon in acts of defence. But since the violence one adopts is *political*, not simply personal, one must see oneself as a representative victim, victimised only through one's membership of a group that is subjected to unjust treatment, or perhaps not personally victimised at all but regarding oneself as victimised because of the unjust treatment of one's group. So one acts as a representative of that group and, insofar as one's action can properly be described as expressive, it expresses the indignation and apprehension of the group, rather than that of particular individuals.

The way of seeing things which is characteristically adopted by the agents of political violence incorporates, then, a powerful metaphor or, as one might call it, a myth. This is not to suggest that it is in any way a *false* way of seeing things. Some groups – gypsies for example – may by any standards be treated unjustly, and there may be nobody they can turn to for help; yet they may see this simply as normal and thus as providing no analogy with situations that occasion spontaneous violence. By contrast this analogy may strike others quite appropriately as the only one that makes sense of their situation and which provides a coherent framework for action within it. Yet evidently, like any metaphor, it may fail to engage, to seem at all apt; and if it does, a resort to violence will look quite unjustified.

The person to whom violence seems, for this reason, to be unjustified is not necessarily engaged in a way of thinking about the situation which is itself non-mythic – not based upon some corresponding metaphor. There is no good reason to think that what I dub mythic thinking is escapable, replaceable with an ostensibly more *rational* mode of thought which does not depend upon the power of a metaphor to justify a course of action. Rather the notion of a rational response, putatively free of the power, dangerously emotive as it is thought to be, of a picture, is one that recommends itself only because of the attractions of a contrasting picture – one which focuses upon the risks of spontaneous action and as a result blurs over the perils of paralysis. Pictures of reflective rather than spontaneous action are themselves various, ranging from those which see the power of a non-violent and thereby ostensibly rational response as infectious, eliciting a realisation of and retreat from injustice on the part of the oppressor, to those which view a violent response as sometimes rational, when coolly calculated in the circumstances to secure justice. Nor do all possible pictures of violence and its alternatives treat the situation as one in which they are responses to *injustice*. While spontaneous violence is characteristically a reaction to the current situation, calculated violence may rather spring from the inviting prospect of some future good than from detestation of one's present ills. This picture in which violence *is* simply a means to an end, a possible tactic, detached from the passions that typically characterise its use in ordinary individual lives, is just one way of seeing one situation, and one which I may reject, not because it seems to me unreasonable, but because it repels as powerfully as another picture may attract.

The point I have laboured is that we fail to grasp the motives of the terrorist, as of any other political actor, unless we understand the picture of his situation that shapes his view of what he is doing in it; the picture that makes it possible for his acts of violence to be heroic, desperate, determined, unsentimental or whatever. I want to stress that the picture which makes such self-description possible is chosen – it is not inevitable, even though there may be no explicit act of choosing between clearly identified alternatives. Choosing a picture in which violence is possible needs to be distinguished from choosing violence within a picture in which it is one possibility among others. The logic of the latter kind of choice – for example the logic of *tactics* – is quite different from the logic of the former.

In order to understand why a picture is chosen we must evidently see it in its detailed application to a political situation. What I have sketched unsystematically have been some of the skeletal aspects of altogether more rigorous ideologies. We cannot grasp the motives for terrorism or assess its justification without some sense of how violence can seem appropriate within them. We need to look at their salient features with the intention of isolating those presuppositions upon which the use of violence is predicated. It is by examining these, I suggest, that the question of justification can most profitably be considered.

ALTERNATIVES TO VIOLENCE

In the absence of operative democratic procedures those seeking *any* political change are frequently faced with the need to adopt methods other than those prescribed for the purpose. But for those seeking constitutional change this is often the case even in democracies. What kinds of non-violent avenue are open to those who seek change under such circumstances and how are they to be compared with a resort to violence?

Evidently we can again distinguish coercive from non-coercive action.[4] Coercive action is designed to so adversely affect the perceived interests of those against whom it is directed that it effects a change in their behaviour. Forms of non-cooperation such as strikes, in particular general strikes, may have this as their *political* purpose. They presuppose that government is in the hands of an interest group which can be directly damaged economically, or which can be indirectly affected by pressure from those who are. Those who suffer the effects of a strike most immediately, however, are not those against whom it is aimed. They occupy a role analogous to that of innocent civilians in war: their suffering is foreseen but not intended. It can, in the extreme, be as great in terms of mortality as that produced by acts of terrorism. Yet while in terrorist acts deaths are usually intended, in strikes they are not. It cannot therefore be argued that strike action is of a piece with violence. It may demand a capacity to harden one's heart; it does not demand hostility.

Non-cooperation for political purposes may well spill over into coercive essentially unlawful disobedience – into law-breaking where it is not some other feature of the act (for example its violence) that is intended to have an effect, but only the fact of its being illegal.[5] How can *this* fact be coercive? It can be so because to defy the law is to confront government with a dilemma: either it enforces compliance or it concedes change. To do the former draws attention to the fact that its authority is under question and that it must rely instead on force. This is politically damaging and in the long term hard to sustain. In these circumstances government may prefer to concede change. What is presupposed, then, by coercive disobedience is that government is in the hands of a group that can only retain its position by force; and that a widening campaign of illegality will eventually break its hold on power.

Why should either or both of these methods be preferred to violence? As long as government is viewed as obstructive rather than dangerous they may well be. But once a conception of the struggle as coercive is entertained then two related factors are likely to decide the issue. First, if a government's response to non-cooperation and disobedience is violent a reply in kind is likely. Second, if a government is perceived as an *enemy* of those whose interests it should defend violence will not be ruled out. The connection between these factors is evident. Resort to violence by the government will naturally cast it in the role of enemy; only the most stringent adherence to the minimum force required for the enforcement of the law and constitution can prevent this. Indeed the government will have made itself an enemy by treating its opponents as one – 'the enemy within'. For it is only a lively sense of one's opponents as part of the same community, deserving of amity even in conditions of competition, that prevents the picture of hostilities which generates violence from gaining a hold on the imagination.

Non-cooperation and disobedience are, however, commonly non-coercive. They aim to achieve their effect by changing the minds of those who can deliver change, rather than by threatening their interests. Thus such non-violent political acts are often described as forms of address[6] or forms of speech.[7] They are resorted to by political actors who are denied effective opportunities for addressing ordinary speech to those in power or to those with influence. As such civil or anti-state disobedience is to be distinguished from a bare protest. For a bare protest registers only rejection. It indicates that the protester believes that what has been done is wrong, but while hopeful for change he may not regard his act of protest as a request or a demand for it. To make such a request or demand is to go beyond expressing one's own convictions. Yet while individual protest may not go beyond that, collective protest seeks a surer outcome. It is enabled to do so by the fact that the publicity sought for such a protest cannot but be interpreted as a way of making a request or demand: collective protest plays that conventional role. There is no way for collective protest to remain bare protest and not to serve as a mode of addressing those in power.

It does not follow that such an address has a single form – that it is, for example, an appeal to the government's sense of justice.[8] Two quite different forms of address may be distinguished. One form aims at persuasion, making no attempt to change the addressee's principles of judgement but trying to show that on them a conclusion follows contrary to that which the addressee has drawn. The purpose of political address is evidently to effect political change. The persuasive form of non-cooperation or disobedience supposes that this can be done by appeal to reasons that presuppose a community of principle between addressor and addressee. Evidently such a presupposition may be false unless, additionally, one assumes a universal standard of rationality even about moral matters. Yet even if one assumes this it is surely implausible to hold that it always determines a way of adjudicating between the pursuit of different interests. There may be *no* principled way of persuading others to relinquish the pursuit of their own interests in favour of those of others.

What the persuasive form of political address ultimately rests upon is the possibility of *dialogue*. By disobedience one makes oneself heard in the expectation of entering a dialogue with government about one's demands. What dictates that there shall be common principles is not necessarily some universal standard of rationality, not even if one is a member of the same cultural community as the government, but simply that both the parties to the dialogue seek a resolution of the dispute via its means. This requires that certain principles be agreed as the basis for a solution. Yet government may lack any intention of dealing with its opponents in this way. In that case if the point of persuasion is to secure what one takes to be a just solution there may be no alternative to coercion. To refrain from it is to be prepared to accept one's situation in a world of unjust men. Its injustices would not be diminished by the use of force, since though force might compel the outcome that justice would demand it would not be delivered through concern for justice. This picture, potent as it is, is unlikely to appeal to someone who lacks either faith in the ultimate power of persuasion or an overriding commitment to abjure the use of force.

The other form of political address aims not at persuasion but at *conversion*.[9] It aims, that is to say, at changing the *principles* of judgement of those to whom it is directed, as no dialogue with them is envisaged, at least until their conversion has been accomplished. A special case of conversion is that of changing the self-interested into the morally altruistic. But other cases involve effecting a change in a group's cultural presumptions, for example of their moral superiority or of their right to use violence. Non-cooperation and disobedience are well suited to secure conversion since they bear witness to the power of their agents' principles in enabling them to endure hardship. Their point, however, is political – to secure change through converting those with the power to make it. In this respect the conversion form of political address differs from mere conscientious objection, in which non-cooperation or civil disobedience simply evince unwillingness to participate in what the objector believes to be wrong. No doubt the objector claims a civil right to conscientious objection, but he may have no hope of securing from government any closer approach to what he believes to be right. Political address aimed at conversion is not content with the existence of separate moral communities. It aims at the creation of a single one, at least insofar as moral principles impact upon political ones.

This picture is perhaps even more optimistic than that presupposed by the persuasive approach; for while that approach could offer some account of why persuasion might work, this picture can only gesture at what are essentially religious views about man's capacity for good. It can offer to the unconverted no reason to forswear violence in the pursuit of justice. Nor is it clear, powerful as the contrary picture is in modern Western thought, that conversion itself should not be carried out by violence – by holy war or jihad.

REVOLUTIONARY VIOLENCE

Non-violence has its characteristic but contrasting scenarios. Those who are committed to it must accept the limitations they impose on what can be achieved thereby. To make such a commitment is to place a higher value on goals other than what one hopes non-violence may (but fears only violence can) achieve. The goals and the permissible methods of achieving them are not sharply distinct. One sets oneself on a certain path to one's goal: following a different route may constitute a different achievement. Just or moral conduct itself may, as I mentioned earlier, be thought to be unobtainable by force. To allow that an act counts as just or moral depends upon the intention with which it is performed and this is affected by the means employed to elicit it. Conversely one may not be satisfied to be *given* one's freedom: one may wish to secure it for oneself; for the freedom that is *conceded* by the powerful may still seem only conditional upon their favour, and therefore not properly to count as freedom. Thus the goals of political violence cannot always be divorced from the courses of action that are intended to lead to them. The question is not 'are these goals reasonable?', 'are these means justifiable?'. But rather, 'is this course of action acceptable?'. We need to look at what courses of action typically fall under the concept of political violence and to look at them in relation to the goals that determine their acceptability.

We are concerned here with principled political action, not with unscrupulous behaviour by agents who do not consider themselves to be justified. Violence and intimidation within democratic states sometimes has this unprincipled character: its perpetrators seek particular advantages while they oppose neither the system nor the way it operates in relation to the policies they resent. But because internal violence threatens the stability of the political community, those who use it from principle must seek either changes which ultimately strengthen communal bonds or changes which sever them in favour of other ties.

I shall term *constitutional* changes which seek to strengthen an existing political community *social* change, and changes which seek to replace it *national* change. The distinction is, it must be immediately conceded, a difficult one to apply in many cases. The basic criteria to be employed will be these: are the current rules determining political relations between members of the community to be changed? If and only if so is social change envisaged. Are the current rules for determining membership of the political community to be changed? If and only if so is national change envisaged.

National change and the way in which it is achieved will be the subject of the next two chapters. In the remainder of this one we shall look at the use of violence in promoting social change. It is the kind of change most commonly brought about by the pursuit of revolution. What relation is there, then, between revolution and violence? Revolutions have two aspects, a *political* and an *inspirational* one. The political aspect concerns the change which is sought in the distribution of power between members of the community and the mechanisms for its control. The inspirational aspect concerns the reasons for which this is sought – the improvement for which a change in the distribution of power is needed. Violence is employed in order to effect a change in the power structure, and those employing it will see themselves as members of a group claiming power or insisting on limits to the exercise of power by others over them. They will therefore view their use of violence as part of a struggle for power. The way violence appears to those who employ it depends on how this struggle for power is conceived.

A crucial distinction here is between violence of the left and violence of the right. The left, as we are using the term, aims to diffuse power, the right to concentrate it. This distinction is intersected by that between totalitarians and liberals. Totalitarians, or those who tend in that direction, aim to remove obstacles to the unfettered exercise of political power whereas liberals aim to impose them in order to protect certain groups or certain areas of life from interference. Though an important feature of the political aspect of many revolutions, this dimension is not a part of the struggle for power which they involve, since it concerns not who wields power but how it is exercised. Rather revolutions typically either seek a change in the distribution of power in order to pursue liberal goals, or aim at a totalitarian system in order to change this distribution. Limiting the exercise of power cannot be an instrument of revolution: extending it can. Both can of course be objectives. But diffusing and concentrating power can be both instruments and objectives. The diffusion of power as an instrument may involve utilising popular action in support of the revolution to demonstrate the accessibility of its goal. The concentration of power as an instrument involves reliance on disciplined obedience to a leader, commonly to secure an analogous political relation as its objective.

Left-wing violence is seen by its agents as *popular* violence, as the violence of the people.[10] This is the case whether or not 'the people' are to any great extent actually involved in violence. For violence is taken to be part of a struggle *for* popular power, and therefore part of a struggle *by* the people, on the assumption that the people seek power. The revolutionary only needs to see himself as acting *as* one of the people, and in this sense as representative of them, to see his acts as part of this struggle. No doubt he will have a more refined view of his relation to the people than this. He may think of himself as part of a spontaneous popular uprising, a people's war, or as a member of a vanguard organisation or whatever. But his justification for violence revolves around his claim that the people have the right to use it in order to gain power. Weighing up this claim is clearly prior to any assessment of whether the left-wing revolutionary *does* properly represent the people and can count his campaign of violence as thereby justified. It is, however, secondary to a consideration of who 'the people' are, of how they are to be conceived as a collective entity with rights and with demands.

This is a difficult question which I shall postpone until consideration of national, rather than social, revolutions in subsequent chapters. It is a question, though, which presses itself upon us when we notice that right-wing, as well as left-wing, revolutionaries claim to be acting on behalf of the people, even though the right wing do not propose to diffuse power to them. Indeed their acts of violence are typically directed against democratic constitutions. How then can they claim to be acting for the people? The notion at work here is of a goal that resides in the nature of the people as an entity, independently of its members' conceptions of that goal. Concentration of power is needed precisely to realise this goal through clear-sighted leadership.[11] Though they do not share in its control, the people participate collectively in the national greatness that it brings.

In this way, perhaps, the concentration of power may be seen as an end in itself, an inspirational as well as a political aspect of violent change. Certainly the diffusion of power may be seen as such. For all competent members of the political community to participate in its use of power may simply seem to be the most just distribution of power, in exactly the same way as the distribution of other goods is, because it puts no one at a disadvantage relative to others in living a good life. More usually and more persuasively however, giving power to the people is intended to secure a *further* purpose. Here we can distinguish two types of purpose as justifying power struggles. One type is reactive. It identifies an adverse feature of the prevailing situation and seeks to remove it. Typically power is diffused to prevent oppression; oppression that may manifest itself in infringements of liberty or distributive injustice. Power is concentrated to prevent decline – decline commonly thought to stem from permissiveness, that is to say excessive liberty and lack of social order, or from egalitarianism. Contrasted with these are proactive purposes which aim at some ideal organisation of society, perhaps a communist or a fascist state.

Evidently reactive and proactive purposes are closely related. But the inspirational aspect of violent political change may emphasise the one or the other with consequences for its supposed justification.

In most of our foregoing discussions of political violence we have assumed reactive purposes. The reason we are, I think, justified in this is that reactive purposes generate a readier justification for violence. The characteristic scenario on the left is the removal of injustice of one sort or another. Other means are supposedly unavailable. Violent change is resorted to from indignation. To resist this justification requires replacing its picture of what is due to people and how they are entitled to act *in extremis* when they do not get their due with a more cogent one, and this would not be easy.

Violence of the right is also fuelled by indignation. But the picture which provokes it has, I suspect, a less powerful hold on most of us. It is a picture of moral decline that needs to be arrested by extreme and urgent action. But the idea that violence against those responsible might be needed, though perhaps once potent in the West and still so elsewhere, is harder to find convincing, conflicting as it does with the liberal view that people's moral standards are up to them: the blandishments and bribes of others, though reprehensible, do not invite violence. But that most of us do not find the picture compelling does nothing to show that it cannot ground a reasonable resort to violence.

Violence for purely proactive purposes attracts similar scepticism. We do not support violence in pursuit of our ideals, in part from fear of violence against ourselves from those whose ideals are at odds with ours. Yet to find the moral fervour that motivates violence chilling is not to show it to be unreasonable.

VIOLENCE OF THE LEFT AND STRUCTURAL VIOLENCE

The most compelling revolutionary scenario of the last two centuries has been that of violence as a reaction to oppression, with the aim of putting power in the hands of the people who have been oppressed. There are two importantly different variants: one stresses the denial of political rights; the other demands a fair share of resources. The former is exemplified by, in the Marxist phrase, bourgeois or, as we may call it, liberal revolution, such as the French Revolution of 1789; the latter by socialist revolution, as in the Russian Revolution of

1917. The kinds of argument for political violence to rectify these injustices are rather different in the two cases.

In the case of liberal revolution the emphasis is upon the claim that the state has forfeited political authority – its right to the obedience of citizens – through denying them either fundamental freedoms or a share of political power. In either case citizens are denied the opportunity to determine important aspects of their lives for themselves: they must do as they are bid or suffer the consequences. The model operating here is that of bondage. Violence is employed to effect an escape from bondage and hence to correct a *wrong*. What is and what is not rightful authority and subordination depends, of course, upon one's theory of a citizen's rights. In the case of liberal revolution it is a theory of the universal rights of man, rather than of his customary rights within a particular social order. Thus, as Hegel said, the French Revolution 'received its first impulse from philosophy',[12] that is to say from an a priori theory of how society should be ordered.

It is important to the theory of liberal revolution that there should be a fact of the matter as to whether one's situation is oppressive, a fact that can be discovered by anyone through a comparison between the situation and what can be discovered a priori as the proper order of things. For this justifies violence on behalf of people independently of whether they are in favour of it or not. The view that violence is justified because people *want* to change the prevailing political order and are prepared to use violence to accomplish this is much less persuasive; for what people want may well be wrong. The political aspect of a liberal revolution is to diffuse power so that people get what they want politically. That they want a political order in which they get what they want politically is a less persuasive reason for their having it than that it prevents injustice. The corollary, however unwelcome it is to democratic conservatives, is that a revolution to prevent injustice may be undertaken without a popular mandate.

The same holds true for socialist revolution. Here the emphasis falls on the claim that the state and the social system it protects have to be changed in the interests of those who are economically and socially disadvantaged under its operation. It presupposes that there is a workable alternative to these grave inequalities and that a change in the constitution of the state is required to put this alternative into effect. Only violent revolution is thought adequate to accomplish this, since those who benefit under the present system will use all the legitimate powers of the state to prevent the required changes, and *in extremis* will not shrink from repressive measures to prevent so-called subversion.

It should be noted that, though the theory of socialist revolutions holds that the present situation under capitalism is *unfair*, this unfairness is principally objectionable because it *harms* people: it creates miserable lives for many which redistribution would avert. While it may be claimed that people have a *right* to fair shares, and are therefore *wronged* by its denial, this is a secondary and optional feature of the theory. If it is adopted, capitalists and the government of the state which protects the capitalist system become blameworthy. Violence against them can then have a punitive character. However, violence against them may, on this theory, be justified even if they sincerely believe that there is no viable alternative to capitalism and are not knowingly guilty of any wrongs against the working people who suffer from, say, enforced redundancies declared to protect profitability. It can be justified, it is claimed, as a response to the 'structural violence' of the system protected by the capitalist state.

The model at work here is of defensive action against the state and the system. No duty of obedience is thereby breached, because the state does not act in the interests of its citizens as a whole, but of those who benefit under capitalism. The state is taken to have a general duty of safeguarding those interests, rather than the limited one of defending rights. This narrow view, it is held, is propagated as part of a capitalist ideology designed to perpetuate the system by securing obedience to the state. Formally, then, the state may act quite properly. But the coercive power it deploys as part of its legitimate law and order function is part of a regime of 'structural violence'. No individual need intend harm to any other nor use force against them except in the pursuit of justice. And yet many are very greatly harmed by the actions of others, and any potentially effective attempt to prevent this is met with force. In these circumstances the system itself is taken to be acting with violence against those harmed by it. It is structured exactly as it might have been had it been fashioned by those who benefit from it at the expense of those it harms. Violence against it is therefore taken to be justified. But, as we saw in discussing the responsibility of unjust states, violence against the system can be nothing other than violence against the individuals who operate it.

How can we assess these pictures of reactive violence against oppression? Evidently there are factual questions to be addressed as to what the allegedly oppressive state does do or could do instead.

But the principal question at issue concerns what the state *ought* to do. And in this connection the question is not what policy it should adopt but how it should be constituted: what ought the state to be like? The revolutionary's view of what the state ought to be like plays a key role in shaping his conception of the prevailing situation as unjust, and hence to be met with resistance. It shapes, that is to say, his reactive purposes, not merely his proactive ones.

A view of what the state ought to be is inextricably linked with a conception of the community that sustains it. Broadly speaking, liberal revolution is motivated by democratic statism and socialist revolution by communitarianism. Liberal revolution seeks a state that at least defends individual rights and political equality, though it does not necessarily limit the state's role to fulfilling this obligation. Socialist revolution requires a conception of the state as serving the common good, which naturally leads to communitarianism. The state is thought of, not as an association with limited aims whose fulfilment produces a community, but as an organisation serving the purposes the community already has. It is the pursuit of these common purposes which brings people together in a community and which is imperilled by the dominance of sectional interests.

The foregoing line of argument clearly does not apply to *anarchist* revolution which seeks to abolish the state altogether. But it is easily modified to cope with it. If one believes that any state tends against individual autonomy or the common good then one will believe that the state ought to dissolve itself. Evidently it shows no signs of doing this, and so one may believe that violence is justified to abolish it. What gives rise to reactive violence is not here a view of what the state ought to be, but of what there ought to be instead of the state.[13]

ETHICAL REVOLUTIONS

Different conceptions of the state and the community typically underlie the conflict between revolutionaries and their opponents. These conceptions are essentially *ethical*: they turn on how people view the good life in relation to their present one. They reflect ethical ideals, and ethical assumptions as to how easily these ideals may be realised. The good life may seem a distant dream of fabulous things, or a prospect of more mundane ones close at hand. To call these conceptions ethical is to presuppose no particular philosophical theory of the ethical. It is to draw attention to such distinctive features of ethical conceptions as that they are capable of arousing passion and in particular passionate attachment. It is an attachment not merely theoretical but practical, guiding the actions of those attached to such conceptions and imbuing them with moral fervour. These are, it should be stressed, *capacities* of the ethical. Others who share these conceptions may simply take them for granted, act on the assumption of their correctness, but with no special enthusiasm.

It is evident that the fact that violence is often justified through an appeal to ethical conceptions which are not universally or even widely shared constitutes a major obstacle to its moral appraisal. It would be comforting to think that there were second-order moral principles to which we could appeal, concerned with the scope and limits of putting a disputed ethical vision into practice. It is hard to see what they would be. What is clear is that none are generally recognised. The situation we are actually in is one in which support and condemnation commonly arise from disparate ethical standpoints.

We can in fact distinguish two kinds of inspirational aspect of violent change.[14] One type, the ethically conservative, makes a persuasive case for change on the basis of conceptions and values shared by, among others, its opponents. The other, the ethically radical, makes its case on the basis of a change in these conceptions and values themselves – on the basis of conversion to them. In the latter case, the political aspect may be unimportant, since what is desired is not necessarily a change in the distribution of power to enable some purposes to be put into effect. It may be instead a change in the purposes that the people within the political community wish to put into effect, arising from a change in their values.

We can distinguish two types of ethically radical political change – those whose inspiration cannot be persuasive without a change of values, and those whose inspiration *is* a change of values. The former is simply ethically inspired revolution, the latter ethical revolution. The former is exemplified by liberal revolution – or counter-revolution in previously socialist states: its point is not to convert people to the ethics of the market economy: it is to introduce a market economy in which incidentally those with the wrong ethical values are disadvantaged. The latter, ethical revolution, is exemplified by, for example, Islamic fundamentalist revolutions: the imposition of Sharia – Islamic law – is part and parcel of the conversion of the people to fundamentalist values, and is not thought of as yielding benefits independently of that.

The ruthlessness of a great deal of revolutionary violence may be ascribed to its ethically radical nature. If persuasion is not possible then all that stands in the way of violence will be some restraints within the revolutionary's own value system. Whether there are such restraints depends on whether his opponents are potential members of his own moral community or whether their failure to be so could be attributed to misfortune rather than to personal fault. In this case they are at least candidates for conversion. If, on the contrary, the revolutionary's view of them is that they are somehow *disqualified* from membership (as, under fascism, certain ethnic groups are) then they will be treated quite differently from his moral fellows. While by contrast if they are thought to have *rejected* membership then they may be subjected to *punitive* ill treatment. In neither case will the revolutionary be acting with the heavy heart of one who resorts to violence *faute de mieux*.

It may, as I mentioned earlier, be hard to accept that conversion itself should be carried out by force, that violence should be directed against those who do not have faith with a view to extending the ranks of the faithful. The object of religious terrorism in such circumstances is to create a community in which the approved religious values can flourish unchallenged. The embeddedness of values within a way of life is presupposed by this, so that a change of values is accomplished by means of a change in the way of life – for example, by scaring Western tourists out of an Egypt claimed exclusively for Islam. That it is terroristic is simply a reflection of the fact that the change has not reached the point where it is the authorities themselves who enforce the system.

Here as elsewhere we should like to get beyond the painful process of putting ourselves in the position of those who use violence from which we would recoil and yet justify it to themselves. We should like to get beyond the process of seeing why from a liberal Western standpoint we recoil from it here – though not, most of us must remind ourselves, everywhere. We should like to be in a position to provide a more general answer to the question: is it justified? Yet no such vantage point may be available. This need not generate scepticism about the point of the question. For within different pictures there will be resources for debate upon such questions. There will be affinities between pictures as well as differences. What these permit is not a dialogue of shared principle. But it is something well short of incomprehension, non-communication and mutual contempt.

Chapter 7

Terrorism and nationality

THE LIMITS OF DEMOCRATIC CHANGE

It is commonly suggested that 'it can never be right for minorities . . . to use violence to try to coerce the majority or the government into submitting to their demands'.[1] The assumption underlying this view is that in a democracy there is always a peaceful method for a minority to have its grievances redressed. Since that is so, the argument continues, violent methods are impermissible. They should therefore be treated, as we have seen, as a political crime.

The assumption is disputable. To start with, a democracy may offer no way of protecting a minority, especially if that minority comprises or is included within a more or less permanently smaller group. This is often the fate of particular interest groups or ethnic minorities. Democracy tends to further the interests of the majority at the expense of the minority. So long as the majority is a shifting one, depending upon the matter at issue, no harm may be done. But when it becomes entrenched within the system even the *rights* of a contrasting minority may suffer. As is well known, democracy is no guarantee of liberalism.[2]

Why do such minorities *avoid* resorts to violence? One reason may be fear: a minority has much to fear from a majority careless of its welfare. If fear is the motive then although democracy provides prudential grounds for avoiding violence, it provides no moral ones. Another reason, though, may be a principled acceptance of majority decisions. Why should such acceptance be forthcoming? Only, it would seem, because one presumes that democracy provides everyone with an equal share in decision making for the community as a whole. That presumption could collapse for two distinct reasons. First, the votes of a permanent minority might *never* have an influence on decisions. It is casuistical to account them of equal weight to those of others. The reason we accept majority voting as fair is because we assume that our votes will sometimes affect the outcome. We are prepared to accept the decision of a majority that goes against us because others will do likewise when a decision goes our way. If we are in a permanent minority, however, we have no assurance that they will act with such reciprocity and hence no reason to accept majority voting.

The situation in Northern Ireland exemplifies this principle. The Republican minority knows that the Northern Irish state came into being because the Unionists refused to accept majority decisions for the whole of Ireland. They therefore have good reason to doubt that a majority vote in the north for reunification – the condition set by both the British and Irish governments for its implementation – would result in Unionist acceptance of Irish unity, rather than in a new secession. They may therefore regard votes for Republican parties as *wasted* votes, so far as the issue of reunification is concerned. The fact that a majority votes for Unionist parties provides them with no cogent argument against Republican violence.

The second way in which democratic voting may fail to satisfy minorities is suggested by this application of the first. It is that, whether or not people have an equal share in making decisions, they may deny that these decisions are decisions for a *single* political community. This may be claimed for two different reasons – because the decisions are for *more* than one community, or for *less* than one complete community. These two cases clearly concern the question of the membership of political communities. Rejecting the presumption of a single political community in these cases represents a commitment to national change, as I have termed it earlier.

It is a reasonable constraint upon voting as a member of any group that one votes with the interests of the group in mind, rather than one's own private interest. Members normally trust each other to do so for the most part. If that trust is breached, particularly by one section pursuing its interests at the expense of the whole, other members may well feel inclined to re-form the group or to leave it. If they cannot do so they are unlikely to feel bound by group decisions which reflect a sectional interest. The point is a familiar one in political philosophy: Rousseau remarks upon

a considerable difference between the will of all and the general will. The latter is concerned only with the common interest, the former with interests that are partial, being but the sum of individual wills.[3]

It is only when citizens aim at decisions which reflect the general will that they are acting as members of a political community. There is only a political community, it may be claimed, when members do generally aim to make decisions which reflect a general will. This will not be so in many of the cases where a minority seeks national change.

It is easy to see that violent revolution might be the only method of securing national change, although the reason is often overlooked. It is a logical limit upon the scope of democratic decision making that the legitimacy of a particular state as the proper body to administer a certain territory is not something that can be established by a majority vote of the members of the state. For what a majority cannot decide is *who* shall vote to decide who the members of the state shall be: 'on the surface it seemed reasonable: let the people decide. It was in fact ridiculous because the people cannot decide until somebody decides who the people are'.[4]

Where there is a dispute over 'who the people are', as in Northern Ireland, it cannot be resolved by the existing membership. The majority in the Six Counties is in favour of the union with Great Britain: a majority of the people of Ireland as a whole would favour a united Ireland. Unionists thus rely on the former majority to justify their stance; Republicans rely upon the latter. But since there is no democratic way of resolving the issue of *which* majority should decide, no argument can be mounted against political violence from the existence of democratic alternatives. It is for this reason that it is in disputes over national statehood that terrorism is so often resorted to. Those who have a grievance over such matters may have no alternative but to attempt to resolve them militarily. Of course there may be secession clauses in the constitution. But these will prescribe voting procedures and so forth that the secessionist minority may not accept, as was seen during the break-up of the Soviet Union. And they might be right to reject them, for, as I shall argue later, there is no self-evidently correct procedure for permitting national secession.

There are circumstances, I conclude, in which we cannot be confident that political violence is unjustified even though democratic procedures are in force. They are normally circumstances in which democratic procedures do not provide appropriate protection for minorities. In these circumstances it is probable that decisions are being taken in the interests not of the community as a whole, but of a dominant group. Then it becomes doubtful whether a single political community exists at all. Where a minority is territorially concentrated it may claim recognition as a separate community. Democratic procedures may provide no alternative to violence in support of their claim.

SELF-DETERMINATION AND VOLUNTARY ASSOCIATION

A minority need not feel it is the victim of *injustice* in order to seek national change. Either a minority or a majority may simply wish to secede – to have an independent state. We may distinguish these two approaches to the question of whether secession is justified.[5] One, which we shall come to later, insists that it is justified only in response to or to prevent injustice. The other, which we shall discuss straight away, claims that the wish of people to secede is a prima facie justification of their doing so.[6] The principal argument for it depends upon the theory that legitimate government rests upon the *consent* of the governed. As Henry Sidgwick observes:

> Some of those who hold that a government, to be legitimate, must rest on the consent of the governed, appear not to shrink from drawing this inference; they appear to qualify the right of the majority of members of a state to rule by allowing the claim of a minority that suffers from the exercise of this right to secede and form a new state, when it is in a majority in a continuous portion of its old state's territory.[7]

Is the inference correct? If it is, then the basis for the democratic state's claim to legitimacy is one that should require it to concede secession. Much political violence is no doubt due to a refusal to concede it.

The idea underlying the consent theory is the liberal notion that individuals should be free to determine their own lives to the fullest extent possible.[8] Any limitations upon their freedom imposed by others are acceptable only if they have been consented to. Thus, on the theory, a democratic state does not have authority because democracy is inherently a fair and equal way of distributing political power, but rather because its members are taken to have consented to it. Similarly, with the state's claim to govern in a given territory, its legitimacy derives from the presumed consent of the territory's inhabitants to membership of the political community represented by the state.

The claim that secession is prima facie justified if desired by a section of a state's inhabitants rests on the inference that they do not consent or have not consented to that state. Clearly it will seldom be possible to produce any plausible evidence of past consent. And even if it could, from generation to generation the actual individuals inhabiting the territory will change, and with them perhaps their disposition to consent. Often some evidence of consent in the form of participation in elections for the state legislature is adduced, weak as it is in view of the fact that voting implies no clearly understood commitment to the existing state structure within which the election is held. Or, by contrast, evidence of non-consent by reason of exclusion or non-participation may be forthcoming.

Let us, however, waive these points and suppose that some argument can be produced for presuming either that consent has been withheld or that it has been granted. In the first case, on liberal principles, the unconsenting individuals have yet to confer legitimacy on some state, and their right of secession flows immediately from this. In the second the issue is less clear-cut; for, if the inhabitants have consented, are they not bound by that act, unless the system to which they gave consent itself incorporated a right to secession should they in future seek it? A marriage, to employ an analogy popular among liberal theorists, is valid only if it has the consent of both parties. But this does not imply that it can be dissolved simply when one of the parties has a change of heart. Perhaps this *should* be possible, but in the form of marriage to which most married people give their consent it is not. Here liberal theorists may fall back upon the idea underlying the consent theory – the notion of individual self-determination – to claim that irrevocable agreements are not binding.

This view culminates in a particular model of the *nation* itself as that which is entitled to separate statehood. For evidently it makes no sense to say that an *individual* can secede from the state, nor does an arbitrary collection of individuals count as *seceding* simply through its members withdrawing or withholding their consent. More is needed; in particular that they form a group capable and desirous of having a separate state. Individuals must think of themselves as members of such a group if they are to act in a way that contributes to secession. They must think of their actions as members as, in some sense, the actions of the group. Let us, without further argument at this stage, call such a group a *nation*. Then the notion that a group of individuals may, other things being equal, secede if the members so wish it implies that they may form a nation at will, and that the nation continues in existence only so long as the members wish it.

This *voluntarist* conception of the nation is what is implied by claiming both that it is nations that have the right to separate statehood – the right of national self-determination as it is called – and that this right derives from the rights of individuals to associate politically as they choose. For if individuals are in no way bound by past agreements in this respect then the nation can depend upon nothing other than their present choices. 'The existence of a nation is', as Renan famously put it, 'a daily plebiscite'.[9] It is a group constituted by a coincidence of wills. It is this view which generates the prima facie right of secession for those who wish it.

The voluntarist model is anti-realist, since for some observers, namely its potential members, whether people constitute a nation depends upon their conclusions as to whether they do or not.[10] Their constituting a nation consists in nothing over and above the outcome of a certain procedure determining that they do, so that whether they do is not, properly speaking, *discoverable* by them. And the model is logically[11] voluntarist, because the existence of a nation is *decided* by its members, as expressed, for example, by their giving allegiance to a certain state. It is the following through of a procedure, not necessarily formal, whereby allegiance is given that determines the matter. Each participant asks him or herself the question, 'what is my nationality?' But their answer is an expression of their will to be of that nationality. It follows that the question whether together they constitute a nation is determined by their will to do so. So their practical conclusion that they do settles the issue, and this is what leads to the model's anti-realism.

It is a fact that people currently exercise their wills in a particular direction. But it is a fact that only *others* can discover. So far as the participants are concerned, what they will is to be determined by an act of *will*, not of *discovery*. And while an individual's will is unable to bring a nation into existence, on the voluntarist model many wills can. So the participants are concerned to bring about what they want, not to find out what the other wants. Their conclusion is a practical conclusion, albeit a collective one.

The indications of national identity, such as a common national culture, relate to its criterion, in two different ways. For observers they seem to provide *evidence* of the relevant acts of will. But for the participants they provide *reasons* for a certain exercise of the will. The same factor may function in both ways. That people live together in the same place may give them a reason for a common allegiance so that, from the fact that they do so, others may infer that such allegiance is forthcoming. Or different factors may function in separate ways. A common enemy may provide a reason for a common allegiance, but is scarcely evidence of it, while actually having a common government is evidence of a common allegiance, although scarcely, as it stands, a reason for giving it. But though the reasons for allegiance may vary it is a certain bond of allegiance which is criterial for the existence of the nation. Perhaps all that we can usefully say about *what* kind of allegiance this is, is that it is the kind for which these sorts of consideration *are* reasons.

How well does the voluntarist conception cope in securing a right to national self-determination? The right to statehood is generated, it is claimed, by the wishes of the nation's members. It is because people want something that, other things being equal, they should be conceded the right to have it. Allegiance manifests a desire to constitute a certain kind of political community – a nation. And allegiance provides a reason for enjoying statehood, since statehood institutionalises the community which they desire and therefore helps to ensure the satisfaction of that desire. For what allegedly confers the right is their desire to live in a certain way, which, other things being equal, makes that way of life desirable and hence a possible ground for the right to its secure enjoyment.[12]

Allegiance is held to generate the right to statehood because the people have, at least implicitly, chosen it. As J.S. Mill puts it, 'one hardly knows what any division of the human race would be free to do if not to determine with which of the various collective bodies of human beings they would choose to associate themselves'.[13] The nation is here viewed as an *association* which people choose to enter.[14] A state is the institutionalised form of this association. But given the kind of organisation the state is, it will perforce be the wishes of majorities that would determine actual statehood.

Yet it is far from clear how the wishes of majorities can confer a right that limits the freedoms of minorities. Even if unanimous allegiance confers the right to statehood, the allegiance of a majority seems hardly to do so. For the right in question is the right of a nation, and must thus surely derive from what brings *all* its members together into a nation. In practice allegiance does not do so, and therefore cannot explain how national identity confers the right to statehood. Worse still, it is, as we have seen, unclear how mere majorities can determine the political organisation of a territory, because nothing determines from *what* population the relevant majority should be drawn. Voluntarism can do nothing to resolve this problem.

STATE AND COMMUNITY

It is apparent that this logically voluntarist conception of the nation, though often promulgated by modern states, does not fully correspond to their actual assumptions. Here two other factors come into play, both deriving from the Hobbesian account of the political community discussed earlier.[15] On this account political association derives not from mutual allegiance within a group,[16] but from common subordination to a state. The nation then, is derived from the state. Second, subordination to the state, once agreed to, cannot be revoked at will. Consent takes the form of a binding *contract*, and the nation consists of all those so contracted. On this model people's willings do not constitute a nation, they produce it. The model is, therefore, *causally*, rather than logically, voluntarist. In consequence it is a *realist* model, since the existence of the nation, once produced, is in principle discoverable by anyone.

From this contractual standpoint secessionist movements are almost always to be resisted as a threat to the integrity of the state. That is not to say that they are to be regarded as arbitrary and irrational. The state claims to rule by consent and while that claim can continue to be asserted against relatively recent, weak or small-scale secessionist movements, it loses credibility where they are widely supported, strong and long-lived. For then the withholding of consent across a new generation, or the competing claims of an alternative state (perhaps with a government in exile) to have secured allegiance casts doubt upon the continued existence of a contract with the state. But it is a state-like political organisation, not simply popular preference, which lends colour to aspirations to separate nationhood.

It is this contractual model, rather than pure voluntarism, which is reflected in the approach to secession adopted under international law. 'All peoples have the right of self-determination', declares the first article of the United Nations International Covenant On Human Rights. That is to say they have the right of independent statehood. In international law the right is generally taken to apply to the inhabitants of existing states.[17] Their right to independence consists in, for example, their right to throw off alien occupation, colonial status or absorption into some other state. These are construed as wronging them through reducing their opportunities to 'freely determine their political status and their economic, social and cultural development'. This legal interpretation embodies a contractual conception of nationhood in individuating peoples in terms of existing political communities as determined by their political organisation. It is evident that this normally does nothing to justify the actual composition of resisting states. Nor in consequence does it provide a criterion for any change in their composition. It seldom provides a justification for secession.

Yet this is a fatal flaw in the official contractual model of nationhood. For if we ask what the idea of nationhood in its political application comes down to, we are struck by the fact that the different accounts seem tailored to suit the political claims of their proponents, which are usually claims to independent statehood. It seems likely then that the modern view that nations have a prima facie right to statehood expresses the disposition to apply the term 'nation' to *whatever* it is that has this right. The view becomes trivially true by definition, rather than one we accept through having an *independent* understanding of the notions of state and nation. But the plausibility of an affirmation of nationhood depends upon the acceptability of the right to statehood which it generates. By this criterion, which we applied to voluntarist claims with indecisive results, the contractual nationalism of established states fails. For the mere current existence of a state does nothing whatever to justify its continued existence. Instead we expect statehood to mirror and to be justified by nationhood. On the contractual model change of statehood (or similar political changes) can bring about national change, but there is no room for the reverse process, which is the one that we expect. Frustration with the use of this inadequate model by established states is no doubt a cause of political violence against them.

INDEPENDENCE AND INJUSTICE

Secession is but one case of achieving independent statehood. National secession implies that the country seceded from is, at least in part, a foreign country, and that rule at least in part foreign is thereby thrown off. Independence movements in colonies or in other countries that are parts of an empire are more explicitly attempts to throw off foreign rule. While secessionists seek separate government, anti-imperialists seek self-government. They seek to govern themselves rather than be governed by others, by alien rulers. This pre-supposes a criterion of who counts as one of their number and who counts as alien. In some circumstances where, for example, the criterion might be thought to depend on racial distinctions, a demand for self-government becomes a demand for majority rule, so that it is no longer *alien* rule, but rule by a minority group, that is opposed. That would seem no longer to involve a national, as against a liberal revolution. Are there, however, injustices against people which provide a reason specifically for *national* independence?

For the group which controls the state to act contrary to the interests of people in a certain region scarcely seems to count as providing them with a sufficient ground for national independence. The case looks different when the *rights* of the inhabitants of such areas are infringed or when equal rights are not even accorded them. Now we have a situation in which they are the victims of discrimination, and so it might be too where only their interests are neglected. We can distinguish cases of injustice arising merely from *unfairness*, so that some suffer harm as the cost of increased benefit to others, from cases of injustice arising from *discrimination*, where some are wronged as a result of a policy of placing them at a disadvantage. I have expressed this as a distinction between being harmed and being wronged; but the distinction may perhaps be brought out more clearly by representing it as a distinction between the mistreatment of individuals and of a group. Mere unfairness mistreats the affected individuals, and what collects them together as a group is simply the fact that they have, as individuals, been mistreated. Discrimination, by contrast, mistreats individuals *because* they are members of a certain group, so that the primary object of mistreatment is the group of which they are a part. Indeed the underlying intention is to place the group as a whole at a disadvantage, though this can be done only by disadvantaging its individual members. It *wrongs* them precisely because they are *entitled* to be treated like anyone else, in the sense that they are entitled not to have their membership of the group taken into account in any deliberate distribution of benefits.

When a group is systematically wronged in this sort of way its grievances may begin to look like grounds for national independence.[18] For it is not simply neglect of which they are complaining, but discrimination due to something which, in the eyes of those who rule them, *already* marks them out as different, either from the rulers alone or from the rulers and others who are ruled. This difference is not necessarily something they have chosen: it is something wished upon them by those in power. Once wished upon them they may accept it as a reason for regarding those who rule as alien to them, and thus as justifying a movement towards independence in just the way that foreign occupation might.

It cannot easily be objected that if the group discriminated against *is* different – and its acceptance of difference seems to acknowledge that it is – then there may be a reason to treat it differently which does not amount to discrimination and hence not to injustice. For the group is governed within what is regarded by those who govern as a *single* political community, comprising the rulers and one or more groups of those who are ruled. To treat people differently in a way that adversely affects their interests on the grounds of their membership of a particular group is simply not to allow them equal status as members of this community, and that is to treat them unjustly. It is indeed analogous to foreign occupation, since in that case there is no pretence of a subjugated people having equal status with their occupiers and for that reason no suggestion that the two make up the single community. Rather, the occupiers are part of a foreign community, and the indigenous community is deprived of the capacity to control its own affairs.

The justification for removing discriminatory injustice by achieving independent government is thus analogous to that for throwing off foreign occupation. It is the justification for self-determination, taken in the sense in which it is a people's right, embodied in international conventions. A national right to self-determination will then be as various in its applications as are the unjust grounds for refusing participation in political communities to groups capable of forming them.

On this account foreign rule need not be oppressive for there to be a right to throw it off. Foreign rule has often been more liberal and enlightened than that by those who shake it off – a fact frequently noted by former foreign rulers. Yet it is one thing to be well treated and quite another to be treated as a political equal, no matter how badly political equals may be treated. Democracy is one way in which political equality can be assured. And that is why independence movements often call for majority rule. But to say that 'there is a prima facie case for uniting all the members of the nationality under the same government, and a government to themselves apart . . . is merely saying that the question of government ought to be decided by the governed'[19] is not necessarily to confuse national self-determination with democracy. For political equality of the sort required for national independence can be achieved in other ways. All that is required is that the *opportunity* for political power should be available equally, in that no one is denied such an opportunity on the grounds of their membership of a particular group of a sort that could, by itself or with other groups, form a political community.

It can now be seen that the right of national self-determination goes with a modern conception of the state that is inconsistent with the possession of exclusive power by a certain aristocratic caste, whether indigenous or foreign, of long residence in the state's territory or not. People demand national change when they seek to throw off domination by such a case, for they seek to change the *criteria* for membership of the political community. They wish, first, that the criterion should not simply be subjection to the ruling caste, with whatever annexations or cessions of territory and people it may make, but membership of a continuing community in its own lands. And second, the community should be a full political community, of which the criterion for membership is common to all participants, not dependent upon membership of a political group within it.

Two consequences relevant to much *international* terrorism follow from these points, one concerned with territory, the other with political equality. A political community can exist only within a certain territory. Thus when rights of national independence are spoken of it is insisted that those claiming the right be concentrated in a territory, that the territory provide for a viable community and so forth. Disputes over secession are frequently territorial disputes. International law is understandably chary of entering such disputes. Instead it operates, as we have seen, on the general principle that claims to self-determination be made within existing borders. The problem that commonly arises however is that these borders have been fixed by foreign conquest and may bear little relation to pre-existing political communities or to possible harmonious future ones. In these circumstances attempts by powerful states to maintain these borders, often by forcible intervention, after the end of occupation or colonisation, may appear as the continuation of foreign domination in determining the criterion of membership of the political community. As such it may attract terrorist responses, in the absence of military force sufficient to withstand it.

Similarly, continuing interference by powerful states in the affairs of formerly dependent ones is resisted as a denial of their equal sovereign status. It is regarded as a perpetuation by other means of the relegation of their inhabitants to second-class citizenship, since, once granted independence, the state itself may be treated like a dependent territory with some local autonomy. Again a violent reaction is possible and comprehensible. In both these cases the specifically *nationalist* motivation is referable to the fact that powerful states categorise others as different in a way that is deemed to exclude them from equal participation in, as we say metaphorically, the *international* community. But individuals have effective membership of a national political community only if that community is on all fours with others in the international state system.

Chapter 8

Ethnicity and national identity

GROUNDS OF NATIONAL IDENTITY

The voluntarist model of nationality leaves it a complete mystery why people should choose, in a way that allegedly generates a right to statehood, to associate with those that they do choose. The liberal presumption underlying the model is that they choose to associate with them because it would be in their interest to do so; it would be in their interest, that is to say, to share the same state with them. On this account, their right to shared statehood may be derived from the right of people to pursue their own interests, other things being equal, on the assumption that people are, at least in general, able to judge where their best interests lie. What might make it in people's interest to share the same state? Presumably either the fact that they have shared interests, interests they share with those they choose to associate with as against those they do not, or a shared view of how to achieve their individual interests. But what, to start with, could those shared interests be?

The problem is to see what kind of fact about *some* others might give rise to their having the same relevant interests as oneself. For it may be taken for granted that everyone has the same interest in enjoying a life of peace and security, the protection of which is the principal office of the state. Our more specific shared interests would, seemingly, have to derive either from the kind of people our fellows were, or from the kind of life they led. The former alternative appeals to the notion of a specific national character, the latter to a notion of national culture which emphasises shared aims and values. We shall discuss these notions later. What we should notice now is that if it is facts of this sort that underlie the shared interests which give rise to national association then it is unclear why these facts themselves should not form the ground for nationhood. For it now seems that a desire to associate with others is based on the belief that there are facts about them in virtue of which they should be fellow citizens. But that, it might be argued, is to ground nationhood not in choice alone, but in a choice based on a judgement as to *pre-existing* facts of national similarity. Then it is these facts which suffice to generate national identity, not the possibly unreliable choices which spring from them.

Similar considerations apply to the possibility that it is not so much shared interests as a shared view of how individual interests can be pursued which explains national association. If, in choosing who I wish to associate with, I am making a judgement as to whether they agree with my beliefs on how that association should operate to our mutual benefit, then it is unclear why this community of belief should not itself be regarded as constitutive of our shared national identity. That might again be to ground national identity in a shared character or a shared culture, now in the sense of a body of common customs and practices, of ways of doing things.

The moral I wish to draw is that voluntarism either leaves the voluntary associations that allegedly constitute nations inexplicable or it threatens to collapse into a quite different model of nationhood – one in which 'it is constitutive of national identity that members of a nation have characteristics which make it appropriate for them to be lumped together politically, rather than parcelled out in some other way'.[1] I shall term this an *ethnic* model of nationality. What produces it is the natural expectation that the choice of fellows with whom to associate within a state presupposes the possession of a pre-existing national identity and hence cannot constitute it.

Nationality can and usually does contribute to one's identity, in the sense of what one takes oneself most importantly to be and what shapes one's choices and actions in such a way that, where change is possible, it is possible only through some perceived discontinuity in those choices and actions. National identity depends, then, on features that one does, or at least can, make part of one's individual identity. They are features which collect people together on a certain scale both in their attitudes to each other and in the attitudes of others towards them. For just as it might appear to be a perception of such features that guides association, so it undoubtedly guides disassociation and discrimination too. In cases where a distinct national identity is *thrust* upon people, through processes of separation and exclusion, irrespective of their choices, it is thrust upon them in virtue of features which they can recognise as collecting them together with others as a certain kind of out-group, membership of which is partly determinative of who they are. Conversely, where the official nationalism of states seeks to include groups who think of themselves as nationally distinct, it does so by looking for features which all members of the state can regard as contributing to their identities as importantly as, or more so than, their smaller group membership.

It is, I suggest, the fact that nationality can contribute to individual identity that leads to the supposition that it is founded upon individual characteristics of, or is at least typical of, members of the nation. The notion of national *character* provides a good example. Features of national society are attributed to the character of the individuals who make it up. Thus:

> In the beginning of the 18th century, when the English were considered a nation more inclined to revolution and to change, while the French seemed a most stable and stolid nation, Voltaire wrote: 'the French are of the opinion that the government of this island is more tempestuous than the sea which surrounds it, which indeed is true'. One hundred years later, just the opposite opinion about the English and the French was generally held. The English were then, and are today, considered – by themselves and others – as a stolid nation, proud in their disinclination to violent revolution: where the French were considered a people easily given to and delighting in revolutionary change.[2]

But notice that the 'stolidity' of the English as a national characteristic consists in no more than the fact that over the last two centuries there has been no sign of revolutionary change in England: it does nothing to explain it. And if one attributes to 'conflicting temperaments or ideals among the masses what were in fact clashes of material interest among rulers or ruling classes'[3] one fails to explain those conflicts. Yet evidently the *idea* of conflicting temperaments, rather than any *actual* conflict of temperaments, may partially explain international conflict. And it does so because citizens of different states *think* of themselves as different.

Notions of shared culture or shared community are replete with the ambiguities resulting from a failure to observe this distinction. On the one hand they may simply involve attitudes, activities and relationships that *happen* to be common to a group of people. On the other they may involve attitudes, activities and relationships *recognised* as common, and entered into with this fact in mind. But this is not to say that what is *taken* to be common must be what is constitutive of a culture or community even though that *something* is so taken may be necessary for their very existence. For without some sense of shared identity it may seem doubtful whether there could be a group with the kind of coherence and cohesion required for a nation, whether or not they have some of the materials for it. This may itself create a doubt as to whether indeed they ever do have these materials – whether, that is to say, national identity could be founded upon *facts* of common culture and the like. It is to the theory that it is that we now turn.

ETHNIC NATIONALISM

The ethnic conception of nationalism, as I shall term it, has two key features. First it is *realist* – it holds that there is a fact of the matter as to whether a body of people constitute a nation, which is in principle discoverable by any observer and independent of that observer's conclusions as to whether it exists. Second it is *involuntarist* – it holds that whether a nation is constituted does not depend upon the will of its members logically or causally. It contrasts in both respects then with what I have termed voluntarism[4] (and in the second respect with voluntarism's fossilised relation, contractual nationalism). The fact on which a nation's identity is based is, under the ethnic conception, not brought about by its members' acts of will. Instead, the acts of will necessary to give the nation a political form ought to be grounded in their apprehension of the fact which makes them a nation.

A plebiscite is thus a very different exercise according to the different models. For voluntarism (and for contractual nationalism), it is a means whereby people can express their will to associate with others, and thereby *decide* which nation to be part of. For the ethnic conception it is a kind of opinion poll to canvass people's views on which nation they take themselves as belonging to. It may recommend itself as a way of discovering their national identity on the principle that people are in the best position to judge their own nationality.

Similarly the sense or consciousness of national identity commonly appealed to as its criterion plays a different role in the two models. In the voluntarist one, the question whether I have such a sense calls for a *decision* on whether to acknowledge this sentiment. Indeed I cannot normally isolate questions about what I *do* feel – for example,

love – from questions about what I *should* feel. In the ethnic conception the sense of national identity can operate in one of two ways. On
the one hand it may itself be a distinct discoverable fact about people that holds them together in a nation, in the way in which a group
of friends is held together by the fact that they share feelings of mutual friendship. In the case of national identity fraternal feelings have
been proposed as the appropriate sentiment.[5] The model operating
here is that of the nation as a family, but one held together by the fact
of mutual feeling rather than by facts of alliance and descent. On the
other hand the sense of national identity may be a *belief* as to *other*
facts that hold members of the nation together – the belief, for example, in a shared history or a common destiny. In this case, of course,
some criterion of national identity, at least for the case of their own
nation, is presupposed. What made people a nation could not be that
they believed they were one, for *what* they believed would then
remain unspecified, subject to neither truth nor falsity. The common
view that people constitute a nation because they believe they do is
simply incoherent.[6]

Ethnic nationalism can be thought to consist in various different
kinds of fact – perhaps in different kinds of fact for different nations
(though there are severe constraints on such apparently tolerant theories.) The key feature is that a nation consists, in Mazzini's words,
of an 'aggregate of human beings bound together into an organic
whole by agreement in a certain number of real particulars, such as
race, physiognomy, historic tradition, intellectual peculiarities, or
active tendencies'.[7] These are the indications of some real classifica-
tion, in accordance with which, according to Mazzini, 'God' – the
philosophical realist's ultimate fall-back – 'divided Humanity into
distinct groups upon the face of our globe, and thus planted the seeds
of nations'.[8] It is God, we may note, or in other words something
other than humans themselves, who is responsible for the formation
of a national group. That is why it is in consequence 'organic', rather
than artificial.

It does not follow that nations are *natural* kinds in the way that zoo-
logical species are. What is *given* is not necessarily natural, that is to
say existing in virtue of facts of natural history. However some theory needs to be advanced in order to explain why what is given is as
it is. The theory that the existence of nations is natural is what I shall
call the *racist* theory. One type of racist theory takes literally the idea
of the nation as an extended family: 'the family is a product of
Nature. The most natural state is, therefore, a state composed of a

single people with a single national character ... for a people is a
natural growth like a family, only spread more widely.'[9] Just as family membership depends on kinship so, it is supposed, does
membership of the nation. One inherits one's nationality from others and is related to those who share it by common ancestry. This is
biological racism, which may be amplified, under the influence of
pseudo-scientific theory into the claim that membership of such a
kinship group can be discerned through the physical or psychological characteristics of individuals, so that national membership
depends upon the non-relational properties of the members of the
national or racial type. There is, however, no such natural typology:
'a racial type ... is simply a combination of averages'[10] in the possession of physical features. What is more those common features
that are *obvious* can in fact mask large biological differences and obvious differences hide biological affinities.

We do not need to pursue the pseudo-science which gave rise to
the eugenic policies of several European nation states in the earlier
twentieth century, most notoriously Nazi Germany. The more basic
kinship theory is apparently more credible though evidently equally
exclusive. Its plausibility depends upon its seeming to answer the
question 'what makes for the identity of a nation over time?'. Its
answer is, 'in the continuing identity of the families that make up the
extended family of the nation'. Nationality is founded on lines of
descent and of alliances contracted in accordance with accepted
conventions. Genealogies and investigation of family origins and
family movements are a natural part of thinking about national identity in accordance with this model of shared 'blood' – a model
analogous to models of personal identity as residing in a continuing
physical substance.

This is the conception of national identity which underlies the
rules of nationality imposed by certain states or aspiring states. Thus
German nationality, for example, normally requires German ancestry, while French nationality, by contrast, is conferred by birth in the
land of France, irrespective of parentage, suggesting a very different
conception of national identity.[11] Conflicts between such conceptions
are evidently political – as is readily apparent from disputes over the
nationality of people of Russian origin in the Baltic and Asian
Republics of the former Soviet Union. But political requirements are
scarcely an adequate basis for putting forward a biological criterion
of nationhood.

A more developed biological theory of national identity makes an

appeal to sociobiology to provide one. Noting that it is between
nations that conflicts commonly arise and that it is within them that
loyalty and self-sacrifice are manifest, some biologists draw a parallel with the behaviour of genetically related animal groups.[12] These
forms of behaviour maximise the chances of a group passing on its
genes to its successors. The nation is correspondingly viewed as a
group similarly constituted and for the same purpose. Accounts of
this kind are deeply flawed. There is, as we have seen in discussing
sociobiological accounts of violence, no way of discovering *which* features of our behaviour have been adaptive in securing our
evolutionary survival and hence which are *biologically* determined. All
we know is that our behaviour has not – so far – been radically maladaptive. Indeed what we do know points in quite the opposite
direction from these claims of sociobiology. First, conflicts between
nations, as we understand the term in a way that makes them roughly coextensive with states, is a modern phenomenon, no older than
these states themselves. Second, such conflict and corresponding loyalty is not peculiar to or noticeably more common in states whose
citizens are genetically related – if there indeed *are* any such states: it
is a characteristic of most modern states, however mixed their populations. If it is replied[13] that the relevant social behaviour is an
evolved trait elicited by those whom we live close to, since they are
likely to have been genetically related, then a biological explanation
of the existence of national formations may have been provided
(though this is open to dispute). The nation itself, however, is no
longer a biological entity: its particular constitution requires a different explanation.

CULTURALISM

Ethnic conceptions of nationhood more commonly offer an account
in terms of cultural rather than biological facts. Such facts can be
either or both of two not sharply distinct kinds: they can be facts as
to shared aims and values, as embodied for example in religion: or
facts as to shared ways of behaving in relation to them – shared customs, conventions or, most importantly, a shared language. The
former valuational facts appear on the face of it to be an important
determinant of national identity and difference. Indians and
Pakistanis, Serbs and Croats, perhaps even Irish and Ulstermen are
apparently distinguished by them. Yet while there may be some differences in the values of the groups in each of these pairs they can, it

would seem, be so slight as to escape at any rate casual detection. Certainly they are not such as to absolutely prevent harmonious relations within a common political community. Rather they are differences of affiliation which are more plausibly viewed as differences of voluntary association whose character is masked by the apparent inevitability of religious conviction. But the conviction that one's fellows are utterly misguided – obscure though this may be to mere observation – requires political separation only within the context of a state which forswears a *national* in favour of a *religious* foundation. Religion is, at least in the cases cited, universalising, transcending national boundaries. It can serve as indicative of national difference only against the background of something else that is shared, as, in the Yugoslav case, the Serbo-Croat language and a host of other practices are shared. For in addition to religious differences these further features are required for any plausible claim to national identity.

In contrast to general values the more specific aims of a group of people may be held to be indicative of national identity. Yet we must be equally sceptical of the claims of 'national aspirations', or 'tendencies', as Mazzini has it,[14] to constitute facts about people which are independent of their will to associate. It is one thing for people to have aspirations that are in fact the same and for this to be a reason for them to associate together; it is quite another for them to have the same aspirations as a result of that association, and it is surely the latter that is the commoner case. When the former is involved it seems most plausible to suppose that it would consist in shared aspirations with respect to making a living in the same land. But this is to shift from a cultural criterion to a territorial one.

The idea of culture as a set of customs and practices, for example the speaking of a particular language, offers a better prospect for providing an ethnic criterion of national identity than the idea of shared aims and values. This is not because values are chosen and ways of realising them are not. Neither of these is more clearly a matter of what is chosen, as against what is given, than the other. We are brought up to value some things and to despise others as routinely as we are taught a language. Rather it is because some kinds of social practice, of which language is the prime example, are more sharply distinguished than any systems of value are likely to be. The reason for this is instructive. We can easily envisage quite different ways of going about things, ways that are initially unintelligible to us and accessible only through instruction. But that we can envisage this presupposes that we understand *what* it is that there are different ways of doing, and this requires that we grasp what value is found in doing it. If there were radically distinct systems of value this would be impossible. It is thus only because people's values differ in merely marginal ways that sharp differences in the practices involved in realising them are possible. If it were otherwise we would not merely feel excluded from their lives by, say, a language that was foreign to us: we would simply not know how to comprehend and classify cultures at all.

Linguistic nationalism is, however, clearly inadequate as a general criterion of national identity. The idea that all those who speak English, say, somehow make up a single nation of people is palpably absurd, appealing as it was, and perhaps still is, to imperialists like Charles Wentworth Dilke, who observed that 'in America, the peoples of the world are being fused together, but they are run into an English mould: Alfred's laws and Chaucer's tongue are theirs whether they would or not'.[15] The notion at work here of language, or culture more generally, as a form or 'mould' is, however, an important and influential one. On the one hand it emphasises the possible acquisition of national identity by acculturation; on the other it implies a consequential loss of antecedent cultural identity. Yet this picture of national identity overlooks the fact that a new language and new customs are likely to be adopted by people who wish to associate with those who already use them. This has an at least equal claim to be what makes them Americans, for example. But it does not somehow assimilate them into an over-arching English or 'Anglo Saxon' nation, any more than it necessarily undermines their antecedent Italian or Chinese cultural identity.

The notion that language or customs are what give people their national identity tends to operate with a very different picture of culture. The picture usually associated with the notion that speakers of German are *eo ipso* a single nation exemplifies this. Discerning 'a complete contrast between the Germans and the other peoples of Teutonic descent', Fichte attributes it to a change of language.[16] This, he continues, 'is not a question of the special quality of the language retained by the one branch or adopted by the other: on the contrary, the importance lies solely in the fact that in the one case something native is retained, while in the other case something foreign is adopted'. German speakers form a nation, then, if and because they are *native* speakers.

A similar criterion can be seen to operate in all or most cases where a linguistic minority lays claim to nationhood. It is not just that they all speak the same language now and are distinguished from others by this fact that is thought crucial. It is that they have continued to speak the same language as their predecessors. The same considerations apply to other practices important in establishing claims to national identity – the persistence of dress, food, drink, song, dance and other manifestations of national or folk culture. It is not that these are different from those of other nations that renders them indicative of a distinct identity, but that they are the same as they have for a long time been. The criterion of identity is associated once again with a picture of persistence over time – in this case one that appeals to, so to speak, a national *memory*. It is analogous to the well-known philosophical view of personal identity, attributable to John Locke,[17] as consisting in the fact that one remembers earlier stages of oneself, each having memories of yet earlier stages (until nothing is remembered in the nascent stage of personal identity).

The national analogue of this theory can take one of two forms. It can either insist upon or dispense with the requirement that the memory of earlier stages in the life of a people is part of the consciousness of its individual members. The folk culture account presented in the last paragraph dispenses with this requirement. It is enough that people continue to do certain things and that the explanation for this is that their predecessors have done them. There need only be, one might say, a *folk memory*[18] of their earlier existence, in the sense that the mere repetition of the rhyme

Ring a ring a roses,
A pocket full of posies,
Atishoo, atishoo,
We all fall down

manifests a folk memory of the prevalence of plague and of precautions against it; facts known to dull scholars, not to dancing children. In the same way language itself encapsulates a people's history in its idioms and etymologies. On this picture, then, culture is not a form or mould into which any peoples can be poured. It is a sealed container that stores a people's past and sets limits to their future development as one and the same people.

The other version of the memory criterion of national identity requires that individual members of the nation be aware of themselves as having a shared history. English law, for instance, requires that both this awareness of shared history and a cultural tradition are needed for a group to constitute a distinct *ethnic* group.[19] But it is unclear why *both* should be required, for if culture functions as a criterion of ethnic identity because it constitutes a kind of folk memory it is not necessary that it should be transmitted through the consciousness of individuals, since if it is transmitted through their consciousness then cultural traditions which preserve it differently appear superfluous.

The shared history criterion of national identity is, then, not necessarily a cultural one, in the narrower sense of having to do with the current sharing of values or practices. But in a broader sense a people's history may be regarded as a part of their culture, and on this criterion it is what individuates a culture as the culture of a single nation: at least some part of the explanation of why they act collectively in certain ways must be that they share beliefs about a common past.

Two versions of the criterion are available. In the first all that is needed for nationhood is that members share such beliefs. In the second what is needed for them to be a nation is not only that they think they are but that their beliefs be true. It is properly speaking only the second version which incorporates a national *memory* criterion for nationhood. But both suffer from a weakness which infects all forms of the criterion, just as it infected the Lockean theory of personal identity. The memory theory presupposes an antecedent criterion of identity in attempting to provide an account of one.[20] For what I remember, or purport to remember, must be that *I* was in an earlier state. Yet the availability of a concept of *myself* as part of the content of my memory presupposes a criterion for applying it independent of its being part of the content of my memory. Similarly, in the case of nations, what is part of the national memory or putative memory is that the *nation* was in some earlier state. Yet this presupposes the capacity to identify something as that nation other than its figuring in national memory.

This is not a purely abstract argument against national memory criteria of nationhood. If we ask what *is* the antecedent criterion of nationhood which the memories presuppose, then it is hard to escape the conclusion that it is a racist one. What it is for some group to be an earlier stage of the nation which preserves a memory is surely to be a group of ancestors from whom the present members are descended via permitted alliances – just as what it is to be the same person resides in physical continuity.[21] This may seem unfair, for is it not true that Fichte wishes to distinguish the Germans from others who are descended from the same Teutonic stock? He employs the cultural criterion of German language speaking for just this purpose. But this reveals that a certain line of descent is a necessary part of the criterion. It is also, one might argue, sufficient. Though he cannot specify *which* lines of descent fall within the German nation and which do not except through an appeal to cultural characteristics, what is essential to being German falls within the former lines and not the latter.

It seems difficult or impossible to formulate a cultural criterion for national identity which does not dissolve into either a voluntarist or a racist one, with their different inadequacies. Just as nationhood has, I suggested, a political goal, so the cultural criterion has, as I hope to show, a covert political purpose.

CULTURE AND POWER

Statehood is the political goal of the nation. But ethnicity criteria seem to fare no better than voluntarism in securing the right to it. First, ethnicity cannot guarantee the conditions required for statehood: a suitable scale, geographical cohesion and social stability. The fact that people share a common culture does nothing to ensure that they form a group on an appropriate scale for statehood. Clearly cultural similarities or differences can be discerned on very different scales: there are no obvious facts about cultures which split them up into state-sized chunks. Or rather, the only obvious facts are those which relate statehood or aspiring statehood to cultural units as *cause* rather than as effect. Similarly a common culture evidently fails to guarantee geographical cohesion: cultural groups, e.g. Romanies, are often widely distributed among others. Thus Mazzini's injunction, 'you should have no joy or repose as long as a portion of the territory upon which your language is spoken is separated from the Nation', is often impossible to follow. And this need not be, as Mazzini thought,[22] because 'bad governments have disfigured the design of God'.[23] What it is to be a group with a common culture imposes no constraint which might fit the group for statehood.

There might seem to be a ready response to this: if the condition of geographical cohesion is not satisfied then redraw the boundaries and redistribute the populations accordingly. But how should this be done? How might culture entitle a group to a particular territory? Perhaps because it is their common homeland. But why should once having had such a land generate a right to statehood there? Only a story of being wronged by expulsion or the like could do so. But this has nothing to do with rights generated by ethnicity. For whereas a people's current right might derive from its forebears', be they cultural, ancestral or whatever, this does nothing to show that a right to statehood derives from ethnic considerations, since the self-same problem arises with respect to how people's forebears had that right.

The condition of stability is not in general procured by cultural identity either. The reason for this is that culture does not necessarily secure the right kind of affinity, unless shared national aspirations are made part of shared cultural identity. For the stability required for statehood must spring from some common interests or presumed interests. Nothing that makes people similar culturally can guarantee this. Relevantly shared values, for instance, need not prevent conflict of interest – they may, as notoriously they did in ancient Celtic societies, produce them.[24]

The second objection to culturalism defining nationhood as what generates a right to statehood is that no mere *facts* of ethnicity can generate a right to statehood because facts can generate no right at all. The existence of some state of affairs can generate no right since all that could generate a right would be the desirability of that state of affairs. Rights derive from normative considerations not empirical facts. It would not be ethnicity as such, as in Mazzini's account, that generated a right to statehood, but the desirability of preserving or protecting some ethnic group in the way that statehood might.[25]

Why have ethnic nationalists assumed otherwise? It can only be, I think, because they have treated it as a self-evident necessary truth that a certain kind of ethnic group, say one with a common culture, has a political function which statehood would subserve. But no empirical characteristics of a group can imply such a function in the sense of a purpose *proper* to the group rather than merely a direction in which it tends. It is, however, only the former that could generate any such right, and not the latter.

If culture, or indeed ethnicity generally, fails to secure the right to statehood required of an adequate account of national identity then why does it loom so large in our thinking about the nation? It is because, as Max Weber saw, that 'it is primarily the political community, no matter how artificially organised, that inspires the belief in common ethnicity'.[26] The belief in a common culture sustains the existing or aspiring political community. A common culture is thus something that is deliberately fashioned or delineated to this end, so that even language, which might at first sight remain beyond the reach of political manipulation, is standardised to correspond as much as possible to national boundaries. Thus the German language that Fichte used as a criterion of German nationality emerged from a range of dialects in the various German states under the influence of German nationalism.

In this case a common culture is designed to encourage people to think of themselves as members of one and the same nation, or rather we should say, to decide to associate together as members of one and the same nation. For there are two ways in which common culture can serve as a reason for associating together politically. First, people can associate thus for the benefits of sharing and safeguarding their culture. This appears to introduce an additional reason for association, and so to some extent it does. But people already have a related reason, namely the benefits of sharing and safeguarding a common *way of life*. What this way of life consists in or even that it exists may, however, be quite obscure to them. To present their way of life as manifesting a shared culture provides a conception of it – not necessarily accurate – that makes it seem worth preserving. Second, people can associate on the assumption, not always justified, that a common culture reflects common interests which political association can protect. This implies that it is a common way of life that underlies and gives substance to a common culture. One way of preserving such a common way of life, and the common interests it brings, is to nurture or impart a common culture.

The political occasion for propagating a national culture that will include those who might not already think of themselves as cultural-ly related is evidently to secure political integration within a state or aspirant state. It is apt for the formation of nations in what are like-ly to be in many respects culturally disparate parts of a territory, for supporting claims to the extension of a territory into areas whose inhabitants are in some respects culturally homogeneous with those in existing ones, and in countering the territorial break-up of the state. This *inclusive* species of cultural nationalism is, I have suggest-ed, a concealed form of voluntarism.

There is a contrasting *exclusive* species of cultural nationalism whose purpose is precisely to prevent the extension of national mem-bership by association. While inclusive cultural nationalism treats culture as something that can be acquired through education, the exclusive species insists on its *natural* growth in those born and raised by certain people in a particular place. While one can, for example, learn the history of a nation, one cannot perhaps feel pride or shame in it unless it is the history of one's *own* nation. Exclusive cultural nationalism sees the capacity for this sort of identification as springing from what one finds oneself to be, rather than from what one can choose to be. If it is allowed to be the latter then it will be 'diluted', weakened, as a source of national strength. We may conjecture, then, that exclusive cultural nationalism flourishes in times of national weakness when what is needed may seem to be strong popular support for the state, achieved by the kind of strengthening of national identity that comes by making it seem an inevitable feature of oneself. Its corollary is the exclusion or marginalisation of culturally divergent groups.

It must at this point be conceded that the contrast is too sharply drawn. For one thing most strains of cultural nationalism will be a mixture of the inclusive and the exclusive. More important, neither kind reveals its character quite transparently, for each depends upon the availability of a civic role that is itself made possible by the state. It suits the state in its aim of legitimation that citizens have the sense of associating freely. Acquiring an inclusive culture is a part of the process of gaining this sense, rather than a consequence of explicit association. Conversely, acculturation of the exclusive sort brings about a sense of inescapable identification whose corollary is an apparently inevitable dissociation from members of other groups. This too can suit the state's purposes. In either case the result is that the citizen slips easily into his appointed political role through acquiring a certain kind of culture.

THE ETHICS OF NATIONALISM

In the last section I hinted at the pessimistic conclusion that it is processes of social control which shape the options of voluntarist or ethnic nationalism, depending upon the political priorities that encourage some developments and discourage others. But is there not, it may be asked, *some* conception of the nation which escapes these strictures and justifies statehood?

Two questions need to be distinguished here. One is the quite local question of whether a certain group, in particular circumstances, is entitled to take such action as is needful for its flourishing, and this may include achieving statehood. Many of the considerations pertinent to this question have already been dealt with in discussing the grounds for justified secession. They clearly include those in which a group has been unjustly excluded from the benefits that others derive from membership of a state and that it can procure only by seceding. Among such cases may be those where the benefits are not political or economic but cultural. That a group values its language, customs or religion is a good reason for protecting them against deliberate or thoughtless attack from a culturally different dominant group. This may provide a reason for secession even if it would have been better for the dominant group to have shown tolerance and respect and never to have provided this reason – even if, in ideal circumstances, there would never have been a need for two states instead of one. The second question is the quite general one of whether an account can be given of nationality which provides a criterion of how, in *ideal* circumstances, the distribution of states should fall.

One possibility to be examined is whether elements of voluntarism and ethnicism can be combined to provide a satisfactory criterion where each separately fails to provide one. Perhaps one could say that a nation is a certain kind of group held together and separated from others by the fact that its members wish to associate together and do so because of the empirical facts that distinguish them from others. Their association is not arbitrary. Thus this account does not leave unsolved the problem of *which* group has a right to statehood, because following *its* will is evidently desirable. This group will presumably be the one most clearly distinguished by empirical facts. Yet these empirical facts are not themselves regarded as sufficient for statehood, since they must be appreciated as reasons for wanting to associate politically.[27]

It will be clear what my response to a proposal of this sort must be. It is that it makes nationhood depend upon people taking certain facts as reasons for political association when, in general, they provide no such reasons. The fact that they are *taken* to provide reasons cannot turn them into reasons. So the fact that this is how people believe themselves to be distinguished in a way appropriate to political association can give no reason for someone to join them in such an association.

The proposed criterion is a species of those that make neither will nor empirical fact sufficient, *ceteris paribus*, for nationhood, but render both necessary parts of a sufficient condition. Yet it is hard to see how fact and will could be composited in this way, for if facts of ethnicity give people a reason for political association then surely they are sufficient to confer a *right* to statehood, even if association is necessary for people to take advantage of this right. On the other hand, if no group of people have a right to statehood unless they wish to associate together, then it is hard to see why any *facts* about their ethnicity, as against their interests, could be needed as reasons for national association, though they might be needed as reasons for thinking that such an association would be politically feasible. But it is one thing to have a reason for thinking one's group satisfies the conditions of viable statehood, quite another to have any reason for willing it. In sum we cannot say that only wise association generates a right to statehood: it is either association, wise or unwise, that generates the right, or it is the facts that would make association wise, whether or not such association is forthcoming.

In general we can conclude that the deficiencies of both ethnicity and association in securing the conditions for viable statehood are in no way repaired by combining them. If the conditions for statehood are met, then the desirability of association required for a right to it is not secured by its resting upon some set of ethnic considerations, however it should seem to the participants. Compositing association and ethnicity cannot identify a characteristic of nationhood in virtue of which statehood is, other things being equal, both viable and desirable.

We can do this, I suggest, only if we move away from the voluntarist and ethnic models and recall that the grounds and limits of claims to statehood must be essentially ethical ones. First the limits: what is right in Sidgwick's suggestion[28] that permanent and structural oppression of a minority sub-group is a reason for secession is that it is a reason for querying the whole group's right to statehood. This is because it wrongs the sub-group. A right to statehood cannot be claimed at the expense of others' rights to the conditions for a decent communal life. And this principle can be applied in the reverse direction. A minority group cannot claim a right to statehood if it occupies an area which is either 'culturally, economically or militarily essential to the existing state' or 'which has a disproportionately high share of the economic resources of the existing state'.[29] It would wrong the larger group to deprive it of the conditions for a decent common life. The principle explains such exclusions to the right of secession and does not leave them as the *ad hoc* result of practicalities.

Clearly the principle is a limitation on any alleged right of self-determination. Self-determination must play some part in allowing a group a right to statehood; for it is hard to see how a decent life would be possible if many of its members had a strong aversion to living together with others in the group. Yet we need to bear in mind here that a strongly expressed antagonism to others may not reflect any practical difficulty in day-to-day dealings with them here: they may not even be recognised as members of the vilified out-group that they are. More basic, then, than formal self-determination is the preparedness to live together with others under common rules, evinced by innumerable activities involving them. If the will 'to join and unite into a community'[30] consisted solely in *such* willings then we might detect it more often than the results of plebiscites would suggest. But, as interpreted by the voluntarist model, it requires more than this. It requires that, as a result of that willing, people *think* of themselves as members of the same national community, and this is not obviously necessary for living a decent life together.

I suggest, then, that the proper grounds for a group's claim to statehood are that it is living, or could live, a decent communal life which would be protected or enhanced by statehood, so long as the life of similar groups is not thereby worsened in a way that they have a right to avoid. The denial of statehood to a national group wrongs it, therefore, by denying it a proper condition for a decent communal life, assuming what would need to be argued, that statehood is such a condition. Since the life of the community is evaluatively characterised it can generate a right, so that the objection to the mere *fact* of communal living generating a right (appealed to on the ethnic model) is avoided. It is not what people do desire, but what is desirable for them, that generates the right, though what is desirable for them is something that they are in a good position to judge. It is also the case that when it comes to deciding what is desirable for them it is reasonable to give them freedom to decide. But this liberal principle that people should generally decide for themselves what they consider to be worthwhile is quite distinct from the principle that their choosing it is what *gives* them the right to have it (as the voluntarist model requires).

These points about the limits and grounds of a right to statehood suggest a model of the nation which would serve to ground the right and escape the objections to the ethnic and voluntarist models. I can only sketch its shape in barest outline. A nation will be a group of a sort, the desirability of whose common life generates a right to statehood. The goals of its common life will constitute a common *good*, for whose advancement it is entitled to independent statehood. What *kind* of group this will be will depend upon what kind of good, if any, we can identify as nurtured by statehood. To answer *this* question adequately the notion of statehood itself would require investigation.

We can note, however, how various may be the kinds of factors which make a life side-by-side with others a *common* life. They may be the occupancy of well-defined territory, or the sharing of a language, or the possession of a common history and traditions as an ever-present background to daily life, or, indeed, of collective loyalties or attachments which suffuse it. They must include some common framework of customary law, or else living together harmoniously would be impossible. Since the primary purpose of the state is the enforcement of the law, it is through this framework that the common good of the group that constitutes a nation is nurtured by the state.

This model of the nation, which I shall dub the *common good* model, may be compared with the ethnic and voluntarist models. Like the ethnic model it is realist: it holds that there is a fact of the matter as to whether a body of people constitute a nation, in principle discoverable by any observer and holding independently of their conclusions. There is a fact of the matter as to whether a relevant community exists and a fact as to whether achieving its constitutive goals is a good. Yet like the voluntarist model it holds that whether a nation is constituted does depend upon the will of its members. First, whether there is a relevant community depends on whether people wish to relate appropriately to others, and second, whether the community aims at the good depends on whether they thereby will the good. Voluntarism does not here imply anti-realism, since the relevant willings of members are not that they should be a nation and thus are not involved in their conclusions as to whether they are one: this is a matter for genuine discovery.

The model allows that facts about people can properly shape their desire for statehood. But this explicit desire may run counter to the implicit desires for common living that they express in a common life. People may just be wrong as to the facts relevant to their claims to statehood. They may get on with those they wish to part political company from. The model has the advantage of allowing nations to develop and change, rather than being ossified in ethnicity. But such changes cannot be arbitrary: they require more than a switch of temporary allegiances; they require a change of life.

The common good model may seem *too* reasonable to correspond to any actually employed in intractable political dispute. But its reasonableness is the strongest ground for recommending it; for, if I am right, the only viable conception of the nation is one that can represent nationhood as a good reason for independent statehood. If so,

the only argument against a clear-headed and well-founded nationalism would be one that attacked the state itself as the proper
institution for safeguarding an harmonious social life.

Chapter 9

Terror and the state

A *TU QUOQUE* ARGUMENT

Many modern states face campaigns of violence from terrorist groups within their territories. All of them, even those the legitimacy of whose rule is obviously open to question, defend the counter-measures they take as morally better justified than the campaigns that they resist. It is the moral character of these campaigns and counter-measures that is the subject of comparison here, assuming that this is distinguishable from the moral justification for engaging in them which derives from the merits of their competing causes. The moral superiority claimed for counter-terrorist measures is supposed to be founded on the fact that they preserve due process of law, while terrorist campaigns are carried on through breaches of it. If due process is occasionally denied, it is only because this is strictly necessary in order that the 'constitution and laws' flouted by the terrorists can be 'restored and upheld'.[1] State action is presented, then, as aimed at upholding the laws necessary for public protection and as conforming to legal processes insofar as this is actually compatible with preventing terrorism. Terrorist violence, by contrast, is represented as deliberate law-breaking that ruthlessly exposes the public to the danger of death and injury which the law aims to prevent.

Against these claims terrorists can mount a number of defences. One is, in effect, a charge of hypocrisy. The state that is being opposed is itself, the terrorist may argue, founded on organised violence; the actions of the state against opponents are not morally different in principle from the actions of terrorists. Such a *tu quoque* argument may take several forms. It may be alleged merely that a particular state which claims to act within the law is actually operating outside it, as for example, the IRA allege that British Security

Forces gunned down three of their members in Gibraltar without provocation or warning. Such an allegation is tantamount to a charge of state terrorism, whose moral standing I shall examine shortly. Or it may be alleged that a state which bases its claim to rule on its authority to enforce the law in fact holds power through an implicit threat of extra-legal violence. But neither of these is, I should judge, the commonest riposte to state condemnation. This must be that the legally sanctioned measures which the state brings to bear against terrorists themselves depend on the use or threat of violence, which is dignified as legal only because the state openly sanctions it. Since this is so, it is argued, there is no *moral* distinction between the actions of terrorists in seeking to gain power and those of the agents of the state in seeking to retain it. Hence there is no *moral* case for regarding the former as criminal and the latter as not only permissible but justified as the prevention or punishment of crime.

This riposte may be more or less limited in its scope. It may be meant to expose the pretensions either of just some of a state's law-enforcement activities – for example those specifically intended to repress opposition groups – or of all, including the laws against murder and maiming which the terrorists break. Or it may be directed either against a particular kind of state, for example colonial ones, or against all states. So long as the terrorist's apologist does not claim that all law-enforcement activities of all states must ultimately depend on organised violence, this assertion is, presumably, an empirical one. We can judge how well it stands up to empirical scrutiny.

We can also assess how well the state the terrorist would wish to institute would stand up to similar criticisms, and make a comparison between the benefits of the new order, less the violence needed to achieve it, and the status quo, including the violence required to maintain it.[2]

If, however, it is claimed that *all* law-enforcement activities of *all* states depend on a regime of organised violence the case is rather different. It is hard to see how this could be other than an a priori claim, and no doubt this is how it has generally been intended both by anarchists, who believe that the destruction of the state will bring about a social order upheld without violence, and by those who believe that while the replacement of one state by another will bring about benefits, perhaps including a reduction in actual violence, it will not lead to the abandonment of all state violence. The two positions come together in Marxist theory, where among the benefits of the replacement of the bourgeois by the workers' state is the possibility of its eventual dismantling, an objective motivated by adherence to the a priori claim. In all these positions the a priori claim that law enforcement depends upon violence is used to deny the state's presumption of a moral difference between terrorist violence and its legal suppression. The question of the relative extent of violence would always arise, of course, although a very determined a priorist might argue that the amount of violence required to suppress terrorists or other opposition must always be greater – though perhaps less evident – than the amount that the opposition that is suppressed involves.

We are concerned here, though, not with these general questions about the moral foundations of government activity or the moral justification of violent opposition to it, but with a moral comparison between them. Yet we can perhaps throw light on the claim that there is no significant difference here without stepping beyond consideration of the activities of the state, by asking what moral difference there may be between, on the one hand, its ordinary activities of law enforcement and the maintenance of internal security and, on the other, those extraordinary activities that go by the name of state terrorism. For one way of viewing the terrorists' *tu quoque* defence is to see it as the charge that the state's activities in general constitute terrorism. Some of them no doubt do; so it is to the question of what might be morally wrong with these activities that we now turn.

STATE TERRORISM

What is state terrorism? On the one hand it has many of the features of war, of a war fought by an army of occupation, say, against partisans, or of a war fought by the state against rebels. The aim of its operations is to remove obstacles to state control of a territory by shooting, taking prisoners, destroying strongholds, cutting off supplies, breaking up command structures, and preventing aid being given by the civilian population. In the course of such operations civilians will be killed, injured, dispossessed or simply terrified. But we need not think that either attacking ordinary civilians or terrorising them is any more essential to state terrorism than to the obviously wartime operations it resembles. Engaged in for the same military or political reasons, these are neither more nor less an objective of state terrorism than of those waging war and so cannot account for its unfavourable moral complexion. What is perhaps particularly distinctive of state terrorism is its use of political assassination, of torture and other cruelties against opponents. Such acts are indisputably contrary to the rules of war, as enshrined in the Geneva and Hague Conventions. They involve deliberate attacks on identifiable protected persons or mistreatment of enemy forces. Such acts occur, of course, in open war, but then they need to be censured or excused by the side that perpetrates them. Their routine and unremarked occurrence in state terrorist campaigns betokens the *secrecy* of the war or warlike activities in which the state is engaged. State terrorism involves warlike intentions which are impeded by constraints from issuing in open war. These constraints are characteristically political rather than military, reflecting, not the military incapacity of the state for open conflict, but political inhibitions in resorting to it. So the intention to achieve the aims of war is usually denied by the state, even when its Ministers indulge in the rhetoric of winning a 'war against terrorism'.[3]

One warlike aim that internal state terrorism does not normally have is the acquisition and control of territory. If it did, it would be hard for the war or quasi-war to be a secret one. But the aim is unnecessary anyway. The terrorists or other opposition groups against whom state terrorism is directed, do not themselves constitute an occupying force in territories claimed by the state.[4] Either because they are too weak, or because their tactics militate against it, they do not provide an alternative government in such territories for the state to overthrow. There are differences of degree here. A fast-moving guerilla war with rapidly changing boundaries of occupation may be little different from a terrorist conflict with none of these. A no-go area patrolled by terrorist snipers and vigilantes may differ from a zone of occupation only in the relative insecurity of its frontiers against penetration by state forces. But there are, in varying degrees, obstacles to control by the state in all those cases, and it is the forcible removal of these obstacles by methods of war that typifies state terrorism.

Yet this, it may be objected, is just one aim among several possible ones, so that the allegedly warlike character of state terrorism is scarcely an essential feature. I do not doubt that there is a spectrum of cases, and concede that it is hard to argue for the centrality of one type. But concentration on other features as central seems to me to distort the phenomenon. Suppose it is suggested, for example, that state terrorism is violence by the government of the state against its political opponents. This fails to bring out that it is not just as opponents of certain policies of the government that the victims of state terrorism are attacked, but as possible obstructions to the power of the state. They are seen, for example, as revolutionaries who seek to undermine the state as currently constituted: were they to gain in strength, civil war could break out openly. Or they are seen as subverting a revolution, which, so far perhaps, has been accomplished without open war, or other radical changes in the structure of the state. Thus the victims of state terrorism under Fascism or Nazism were officially portrayed in the former light – as violent communists – while they might more accurately be viewed in the latter.[5] The motive that might lead to war, and some of its corresponding methods, are present. Or, if the motive is absent, it is at least feigned as a cover for attacks on political opponents, who can be represented as enemies of the state.[6]

So far I have attempted to establish an affinity between state terrorism and war. I have said little about the differences. I have noted, however, that state terrorism normally operates in areas where there is no governmental structure able to enforce order but the state's, and that is being challenged. Perhaps there are no structures with that capacity at all. In these circumstances, there is a strong temptation for the state to engage in state terrorism to re-establish its control; for if it engages in open war then it appears to concede its incapacity to enforce the law in terrorist areas, either wholly or in respect of terrorist crimes. In order to maintain its credibility as the ruling power there, the state will naturally purport to be operating within the framework of the law which it presents itself as upholding. If, however, it is unable to resist terrorism within this legal framework it may resort to the covertly warlike operations which constitute state terrorism. It is evident that such a sequence of events is commonplace. Under-cover soldiers in Northern Ireland, purportedly acting to give Military Aid to the Civil Power, have frequently disclosed that they 'took out' terrorist suspects without legal niceties. What is it that inclines us to call this state terrorism, rather than straightforward war?

It is not, as I have already suggested, that it is contrary to the rules of war, for were there to be an open war such attacks on enemy forces would be permissible. Even rules that require the taking of prisoners rather than the killing of troops who are militarily incapacitated are relaxed in the case of non-uniformed troops – as terrorist units tend to be. However, the abandonment of uniforms by either side in terrorist conflicts is an indication of their unwillingness to be bound by the usual rules of combat. But given that the rules of war are not in force, the ordinary rules of civil life ought to be. What makes the 'taking out' of terrorists without due process of law state terrorism is that it violates these rules.

One way, then, in which state terrorism can occur is through the law being breached by murder, malicious wounding, kidnapping and similar crimes being perpetrated, albeit by the agents of the state and in pursuance of state policy. There are ways in which terrorists can legally be killed or wounded, if, for example, they do not heed warnings to give themselves up when detected in the commission of a crime, or they can be captured, so long as it is by way of a legal arrest. If terrorists are denied due process of law, then the same acts are criminal, even though in open war they would have no such character. Acts of this sort perpetrated by agents of the state in a secret war or near-war seem to me to be of the essence of state terrorism, though this claim will require some qualification.

This account has the advantage, however, of identifying state terrorism as a species of terrorism in general, of which anti-state terrorism is another species. Terrorism is, in general, I have argued, characterised by the intention to wage a war: the terrorist must, allowing for marginal cases, have that kind of attitude and aim with respect to his opponents that makes them enemies to be defeated. It is not only anti-state terrorists who have such intentions, so accounts of terrorism as 'revolutionary violence' are inadequate.[7] The terrorists' intention to wage a war is, however, frustrated by a variety of constraints, so that the war or near-war is a secret or extremely limited one. Yet what makes anti-state hostilities terrorist is that they are treated by the state as criminal. This is one way in which the anti-state terrorists' intention to wage war can be systematically frustrated by a state which refuses to make a military response. One can say similar things about pro-state or state terrorism. Pro-state terrorism is evidently outside the law even if the state does not proceed against its perpetrators. It is not legitimised by being made part of a war conducted by a state which gains the covert aid of irregular forces. State terrorism too is characteristically criminal. It takes place before a background of law-enforcement activities against insurgents or other opposition groups, so that even though it is perpetrated by agents of the state and perhaps even acknowledged by them, it is contrary to the laws enforced by the state elsewhere and, as such, criminal.

The crucial point here is that what makes terrorism criminal is that it is, in its context, in breach of the ordinary domestic civil laws. Does this feature of criminality provide us, then, with an easy answer to the question we posed earlier: why is state terrorism wrong? Unfortunately it does not, and for two reasons that shed a morally unfavourable light on state terrorism.

First, and quite simply, the criminality of terrorism in general does not show that it is morally wrong. If we assume that killings in wartime may in certain circumstances be morally permissible then it is hard to see how acts of terrorism committed in similar circumstances may not be. For if the mere fact that the latter were treated as criminal by the state could change their moral complexion then the moral properties of these acts could depend simply on whether the state responded to them by military or by legal means. It is difficult to see how whether these acts were morally permissible or wrong could depend simply on that, in advance, perhaps, of their agents knowing what the response of the state might be. Admittedly a moral obligation to obey the law might be adduced as what makes otherwise morally permissible acts impermissible.[8] But it is not a breach of this defeasible obligation that accounts for the moral wrongness we often attribute to terrorism. Rather it is that it involves acts that are in themselves morally impermissible, save in the exceptional circumstances of war, but that we do *not* discern as having such exculpating circumstances. My point is merely that the *state's* refusal to treat these acts as acts of war by treating them as criminal cannot settle whether they are rightly so regarded morally.

Yet similar remarks cannot be made about state terrorism. If an act of state terrorism were morally permissible as an act of war then the state should acknowledge it as war. If it does not, it can scarcely secure the justification that acts of war can have. For this depends upon being able to make a distinction between what is and is not militarily necessary for certain objectives of combat.[9] Even if a state acknowledges that it is fighting a war its acts will lack justification if it does not observe this distinction. If the state refuses to concede that it is engaged in combat at all its operations would not normally be circumscribed by concern for this distinction. It would then be by chance and not design that certain operations would, in a context of open war, be morally permissible.

It is the refusal to acknowledge that a war is being fought which leads to the violations of its rules in state terrorism noted earlier. Unlike the anti-state terrorist (or even the pro-state terrorist) the state terrorist cannot seriously claim to be fighting a war. Perhaps one should say, he cannot admit to it. If he did his actions would no longer, other things be equal, count as terrorism, for the general reasons cited earlier. Of course the *rhetoric* of war can be used, as by Italian Fascists and German Nazis in the 1920s and 1930s.[10] But a serious claim to be engaged in war rather than, say, political liquidation or genocide requires *some* operative conception of military necessity. Yet in the case of anti-state terrorism we can equate the state's refusal to regard it as war with the state's treatment of it as criminal. We have already seen that the state's refusal to acknowledge its own activities as war does not require it to *treat* these activities as criminal, even if they count as such by laws enforced elsewhere. We should now note, and this is the second reason for rejecting the suggestion that state terrorism is morally wrong because criminal, that state terrorism may not even count as criminal.

The state may, and fascist states habitually do, legitimise their violent acts of oppression against opponents by passing laws that permit summary execution, torture or detention without trial. We could hardly suppose that their moral complexion is at all affected by this fact. The reason for regarding such acts as morally wrong is quite independent of whether the state turns a blind eye to them or openly legalises them, though the latter may constitute an additional moral evil. Nor do we want to say that whether acts count as state terrorism is affected by the mere fact that they are legalised. This is the qualification needed to augment my claim that terrorism has an essentially criminal character. The state can legalise its own terrorist acts while they remain terrorist, because they do not occur as part of an openly acknowledged war. They still count as terrorist, we might say, because they involve, simply to serve state policy, breaches of rules we expect, in those circumstances, to be expressed in law.

The qualification to our account is not, then, a radical one. Terrorism which is legalised by the state involves making exceptions to laws which protect citizens in times of peace from being killed, wounded or imprisoned without the application of recognised legal processes. Acts of legalised terrorism thus constitute a grave infringement of human rights. In such cases it may be argued that, although legislation has been carried through which is technically in order, the fact that it breaches human rights invalidates it under international law – *lex iniusta non est lex*.[11] In that case foreign courts would not recognise the acts as lawful and domestic or international courts might subsequently try their perpetrators for crimes of murder and so forth. We shall need to look at such a contention more closely later. Meanwhile we should note a corollary to it. It is that those who engage in legalised state terrorism cannot shelter from individual punishment on the grounds that their acts are 'acts of state'. They will be so no more than if their acts were contrary to the law, though smiled on by the state.

This brings us to the critical point about the criminality of state terrorism, namely that it is only in an extended sense that acts of state terrorism are acts of state at all. A criminal act by an agent of the state is, normally, only the private act of an individual. As Henry Sidgwick puts it 'it seems most simple and logical to lay down that an official acting illegally loses all advantage of his official character, so far as this action is concerned'.[12] There are exceptions, as when laws are broken inadvertently but without negligence. When a miscarriage of justice, for example, results from *criminality* on the part of state officials, the suppression of evidence, say, or the beating up or drugging of the accused, as apparently happened in the case of the Guildford Four, the state, it is true, is expected to take responsibility for the consequences of the acts of its agents. Were it not to do so there would be a suspicion that it renounced *control* over agents of the executive. But none of this shows that the state is itself responsible for the performance of its agents' acts.

Paradoxically then the paradigms of state terrorism are the *private* acts of those who happen to hold state office and, for that or other reasons, stand to benefit from the preservation or extension of the state. This is due to what is additionally wrong with it, over and above what may be wrong with it as an instance of terrorism. It is the abuse of state power for private, albeit political, ends. It is, as such, inherently tyrannical. Since it is tyrannical, Mill maintains that the 'act of a private citizen in striking down a criminal, who by raising himself above the law, has placed himself beyond the reach of legal punishment or control . . . is not of the nature of assassination but of civil war'.[13] State terrorism is, of its essence, something to be opposed.

THE STATE AND SECURITY

The upshot of the preceding discussion is that state terrorism can scarcely serve as a suitable model for the acts of the state which do employ violence against those who threaten its security or order. The trouble with directing a charge of state terrorism against the state's counter-terrorist operations, as part of a *tu quoque* argument, is that state terrorism is *worse* than terrorism, not simply, other things being equal, of the *same* moral complexion. But this conclusion will only follow if we can find a coherent conception of state action which provides some indications of where the proper limits of state action lie. Otherwise terrorist and state violence will be on all fours.

What is required for the notion of acts of state is, of course, the idea of a *constitution* within which such acts are performed. The primary rules or laws enforced by the state must be promulgated and administered within a framework of secondary rules. These do not merely *regulate* the actions of a state. They *constitute* certain kinds of law-enforcing activity as acts of the state.[14] But if a coherent concept of state action is thereby introduced there must be a clear distinction between conforming to secondary rules correctly and merely seeming so to do. They must, in other words, exert real constraints on those whose actions are constituted as state actions by them. It follows that an act cannot become an act of state simply by conforming to the will of a dictator, for there would then be no difference between an act of state and his private act. The necessary constraints of secondary rules would be absent. If, therefore, Himmler's deputy, Werner Best, was attempting to report the constitutional position in Nazi Germany when he said, 'As long as the police is carrying out the will of the leadership, it is acting legally',[15] then he must have been wrong. For in these circumstances it would not have been possible for members of the police force to operate as properly constituted agents of the state at all. Still less could their position put them above the law to which other citizens were subject; since only if they were acting as agents of the state could they act under those exceptions to the law which allow for the police to shoot those resisting arrest and to engage in other violent acts forbidden to ordinary citizens.

So far this account of what constitutes state action is schematic and insubstantial. Yet it suggests a model of the state as a body whose essential purpose is to enforce laws or primary rules, and whose constitutional or secondary rules provide for it to do so. It would not follow that *all* secondary rules were directly concerned with law enforcement. But if we wish to seek some limits as to which rules can properly be regarded as constitutive of state action, then we shall look to law enforcement as the purpose of the state.

Evidently this position is open to a number of challenges. One is the claim that 'There cannot be a satisfactory "substantive" definition of the political because political organisations, including States, have been concerned with all sorts of different activities. . . . The only feature which all political groups have in common is the means they employ, namely the use of force'.[16] A second challenge would *extend* the purpose of the state beyond law enforcement, so that 'its primary function is to settle and prevent conflict or to put it another way, the keeping of order and the maintenance of security', where the former is accomplished by enforcing the law, the latter by the maintenance of armed forces, etc.[17] Other challenges may discern other purposes, but I shall not be concerned with them. As to the first challenge, I say only this. I do not see how secondary rules constituting state action could be picked out only by reference to a *method* of doing things, even if the method – namely the use of force – is one to which the state claims a monopoly. The whole point of this claim is to establish that only the state's use of force is *legitimate*. But for that it must surely be used, ostensibly, for certain *purposes* which allegedly legitimise it. Secondary rules, as I have introduced them, must specify a method for attaining these purposes, namely the state's method. The purpose may be to regulate the use of violence, and only counter-violence may be a suitable method for attaining this end. But in that case some 'substantive' definition of the political has been found.

The second challenge accepts that the state has a purpose, broadly the protection of citizens, but sees this as having what are normally internal and external aspects, inasmuch as the threat is from within the citizenry or from without, namely the preservation of order and the maintenance of security respectively. The enforcement of law is seen as just as contingent to the character of the state as the maintenance of armies is. Force is here in no way essential to the state. I have argued that this commonplace picture is erroneous. However the first point to reiterate is that the notion that law is only contingently necessary to the existence of a state is quite implausible. A body which maintained order within a territory by drugging the population would not thereby have become the state apparatus. Drugging an *enemy* population would, by contrast, be a possible way in which a *state* could act, to maintain security. The point has nothing to do with the liberties of or duties to citizens. It is just that it is only by enforcing law that the keeping of order in general counts as the action of a state, rather than some other kind of political organisation.

The maintenance of security is – as I have argued earlier – the securing of territory within which order can be kept by enforcing the law. Incursions from without are threatening to the state because its citizens are exposed to attacks which cannot be prevented or punished at all or, if the incursion is successful, can only be prevented or punished by another state. Insofar as a given state has responsibility for enforcing a body of laws which *inter alia* prohibit attacks on citizens, the result of these incursions is that the state can no longer fully carry out its responsibilities. I do not then see the maintenance of security as a purpose distinct from law enforcement, but rather as a purpose subsidiary to it.

The maintenance of security is not in itself constitutive of the state. The only plausible way to present it as such is to link it with the preservation of order under the umbrella of protecting the citizens, but that I have demurred at. (One might add that there are all sorts of other forms of protection of the citizen that states may or may not go in for, but which nobody thinks are constitutive of them.) What nobody could plausibly argue is that the maintenance of the state *with its existing borders and internal structure* is a purpose constitutive of the state, although that is what is often meant by the maintenance of national security.[18] The reason is obvious: this statement of a constitutive purpose would already presuppose a prior understanding of what does constitute the state. We do have here, however, a purpose that state action often serves and is designed to serve, namely the maintenance of a particular state structure, of which the particular boundaries are but one aspect. Such a purpose will inevitably be served to some extent *whenever* the state acts to preserve its apparatus for enforcing law in a territory. It is, as I shall try to bring out, important to distinguish these purposes: the latter derivative from what is constitutive of the state; the former purely contingent and able to be served by the state, rather than by private groups or individuals, only in virtue of the availability of actions that serve the latter purpose.

THE FORCE OF LAW

We can, I have suggested, draw a principled distinction between state terrorism and coercive acts by the state which subserve its constitutive purpose of law enforcement. Does this, however, turn aside the terrorists' *tu quoque* argument that state violence is morally no better than terrorist violence? There are two questions here, depending upon the intended scope of the argument. One asks whether the fact that the state's use of force is to enforce the law improves its moral complexion in general. Might not law enforcement, while constitutive of the state, still function as a device for retaining power? The second asks merely whether the fact that the state uses violence to enforce the law *against terrorists* improves its moral complexion as against theirs? Might not *this* use of the law be no more than a device for retaining power, while not being *required* by the purposes constitutive of the state? It is the second more modest question that I am principally concerned with here. But in order to tackle it I shall need to make some remarks which may go some way towards suggesting an answer to the first. Two models of the law which relate to the communitarian and statist views of political society discussed earlier need recapitulating here. We may call one *normative*. It locates the ultimate authority of the law in its expression of moral principles, principles as to how to live well in a community. In ideal circumstances social life would be guided by these principles without requiring the sanction of law enforcement. Only in specific historical circumstances is the apparatus of a state needed to perform this task on behalf of society. The state's role then is to exercise a responsibility to society. Conversely citizens owe a duty of support to the state that enforces their laws. In sharp contrast to this is the *positivist* model of law, which locates its ultimate authority in the power of a state apparatus to enforce it. Left to themselves people would be embroiled in the Hobbesian 'warre of every man against every man'. Only through its superior force is the state able to control them and make them conform to laws which prohibit attacks and other harms.

Let us first ask, then, whether, if the normative model were correct, the state's enforcement of the law against terrorists would exemplify the fulfilment of its obligations to its citizens. If it did, then it might be morally different in kind from the terrorism it suppresses. At first sight it will seem as if this is the case. The laws the state enforces against terrorists are just those against murder, wounding, kidnapping, etc. which reflect the community's rules. Surely these should be applied impartially to protect all citizens. Whatever the motives of the terrorists, have they not committed crimes against the community? The matter is not so simple. In the normative model no simple equation is possible between offences against the state and offences against the community, as is implied in the notion of a *public* wrong as 'an offence committed against the State or the community at large'.[19] For when the responsibility for taking action is put into the hands of a state apparatus, offences against the state become possible that may have no tendency to subvert the rules of the community in general, for example, acts against agents of the state who enforce laws not recognised by the community, or who in other ways act oppressively.

The normative model is able, then, to differentiate what is owed to the agents of the state when they are acting otherwise than to enforce the laws of the community, from what is owed to its ordinary members. Of course it must accept that the state needs to retain the powers necessary for enforcing the law, but it can distinguish actions done to this end from those which aim rather to preserve the existing state structure, because it benefits those who hold power under it. The normative model in no way prohibits such actions, but it cannot recognise them as the enforcement of the community's rules. It is, of course, the existing state structure which terrorists threaten and which the state seeks to preserve in resisting them. So long as it is only the agents of the state who are attacked with this end then it is hard to see why the community should require the law to be enforced against their assailants. Rather it will expect to be given the kind of protection from the consequences of attack that a state provides by armed resistance. In a war the community demands to be spared direct attacks, since it is not the community but the state which is a party to the conflict. But, for the same reason, the community does not, other things being equal, require that it be given the protection of arms, rather than the protection afforded by cession to the enemy, or, one might say, a political settlement.

There are difficulties in applying this fundamentally pre-modern theory to the conditions of a modern state beset by terrorism, where, as I have mentioned, there are no clear lines between opposing forces, behind which law and order can be maintained. In this situation it may be difficult to see how the state can fulfil its law-enforcement obligations while fighting a war. It can surely always plead that it is defending itself simply to retain the power to do that. But the obligation to ensure that there is *some* such power is not the obligation to preserve the power involved in a *particular* state structure. At specific times and places it will be difficult to judge which aim is being pursued. It is, of course, very much in the interests of a particular state to blur the distinction between these aims and present its application of the law as required of it by its obligations to the community. If, as I suspect, it frequently is not, then even assuming that the normative model of law is right, the terrorists' *tu quoque* argument against the state's claim to moral superiority in the use of violence has considerable force.

Contrasting with the normative model of law is the positivist one which sees laws as the commands of the state to its citizens backed by threats of violence, imprisonment or forfeiture. Laws are required to contain conflict between citizens, but do so only by inducing potential conflict between the citizens and the state, in which the state will have the power to impose its will. On this model the terrorists' *tu quoque* argument may look impregnable: superior power cannot confer moral superiority. In fact, it is still necessary to distinguish law enforcement from other coercive acts of the state and assess the proper scope of each in relation to opposition. Does its use of the law against terrorists give the state a moral advantage?

Evidently the state will claim that it does. Its use of power to enforce laws which prevent societal conflict is, it will allege, morally different from the use of power to control the members of society in a way which serves the interests of those wielding power. The former has a utilitarian justification in terms of the net balance of benefits and harms it produces. The latter would be motivated by concern for sectional rather than general interests. By this measure, the state's ordinary activities come out as morally superior to the terrorist's. What is more the terrorist's acts are rightly treated as an aberration to be dealt with, if possible, in accordance with legal procedures. For the benefits of peace are thereby maximised and harm, including harm to the terrorist himself, is minimised.

This argument would have considerable force if its utilitarian justification for law enforcement could be accepted. But this is precisely what the terrorist himself is likely to question. The particular state structure he challenges is not, he will suggest, as disinterested as it claims. The regime he wishes to introduce would be morally superior. For this reason he will view the state's use of the law against him as a cover to disguise the real motivation of power retention in the hands of a currently dominant group.[20]

My conclusion is dispiritingly sceptical. It is that no good arguments seem readily available to back up the state's repudiation of the *tu quoque* argument addressed by the apologists of terrorism. The state's claim to moral advantage in maintaining its role of law enforcement does not yet seem compelling. My argument has been that law enforcement itself is not as such a use of violence comparable to that of terrorists. But the use of force necessary to maintain the law-enforcement function is. Just as there is commonly no alternative to a resort to violence in pursuit of the terrorist's aims, so there is usually no alternative to it in the state's maintenance of power – of what is known as national security. Yet, while a political opponent can choose not to use violence in support of his cause, the state cannot renounce force while maintaining its claim to responsibility for law enforcement. The fact that this use of force bolsters the existing state structure must cast doubt on the state's response to the terrorist's *tu quoque* argument: that its use of force is different in kind from his because it is necessary for maintaining order. This does not, of course, imply that for the state anything goes, that no distinction can be drawn between its use of reasonable force and its resort to intolerable violence.

Chapter 10

The violence of the state

GROSS HUMAN RIGHTS VIOLATIONS

Almost everywhere and at almost all times citizens who oppose the will of their rulers are liable to be imprisoned, tortured or killed. We are nonetheless horrified and outraged by this, as perhaps people in other places and at other times have not been. We seek an explanation, in the hope that it may lead to some way of alleviating these ills, though others, perhaps, sought none, and entertained no hopes of amending the conduct of powerful and evil people. So what *kind* of explanation might we seek of a phenomenon that is as pervasive as is the violent treatment of political dissentients by the state? Clearly that it is all too common does not make it comprehensible. But we need to understand how what has perhaps been treated as comprehensible just because it has been so common can come to appear otherwise. For this change is closely connected with the development of expectations about how we might ourselves reasonably be treated if we were dissentients. It is in the light of this that what may continue to be common practice can now seem to be a flagrant breach of what is due to citizens, and not just a brutal exaction of what is due from them. In a word, it can seem to be a violation of their rights. Thus it is against the background of regarding a respect for rights as *normal*, not of the *typical* practice of brutality, that we seek an explanation of violations.

I want to provide a context of this kind for our horror-struck and probably helpless question, 'Why do these things happen?' since unless we bring these acts under a specific description no explanation of them is possible. Our question must have the form: 'Why are there things falling under *this* description?' It is only if we find a description under which things call for an explanation, as surprising,

shocking or otherwise contrary to some kind of reasonable expectation, that we will know where to look for one. And, in the horror of
brutal violations of people's rights, the helplessness of our question,
'Why do these things happen?' often reflects our own difficulty in
specifying just what description of the events disturbs our sense of
what is to be expected. So one more specific question that is possible
might be: 'Why do their rights afford them no protection here?' For
since we may reasonably expect them to be so protected the violation of rights provides a description under which these acts call for
explanation.

We need to appreciate how very different such an explanation
must be from that we seek if we are struck by the initially inexplicable cruelty or callousness of the violation. 'How can anyone be so
cruel?' is a quite different question from 'How can anyone fail to
respect these rights?' and the first question may be the right one. For
the cruel and the callous do not act under the description 'violating
a right', any more than someone who walks down the street normally acts under the description 'exercising a right'. Such a
description is simply irrelevant to the purpose of the act. So for that
reason the question 'Why do they violate these rights?' will equally
be irrelevant. It will be no more relevant now, when it is generally
accepted that people have (as stated by the UN Declaration of
Human Rights) 'the right to life, liberty and security of person' which
would be violated by 'torture or . . . cruel, inhuman or degrading
treatment',[1] than when such rights were not generally conceded.
There may now be the question 'Why does the existence of these
rights not deter the torturer?', but the question why such cruel acts
as torture occur is, it would seem, a more ancient and abiding one.

I wish to suggest, then, that, when we seek an explanation of gross
human rights violations, we may be interested not so much in their
character as rights violations but in their *grossness*. This, it seems to
me, is not a measure of the extent to which a person's rights have
been violated, but rather of the degree of cruelty or callousness
evinced by violation. Human rights are many and varied.
International declarations and conventions assign many rights – like
the right to rest and leisure[2] – which many countries do, perhaps can
do, nothing to protect, and which they may even act to undermine.
But violations of such rights, however extensive, cannot be gross.
Indeed we might more properly speak of a *denial* of rights here, since
they require that certain things be done for us, not that certain things
not be done against us. What makes us identify some rights – those

to life, liberty and security of person – as ones which can be grossly violated is that attacks on life, liberty and the person are already seen as glaring ill-treatment. They are seen as such even outside the framework of expectations of good treatment which give rise to the ascription of rights. So when we come to think in terms of rights we assign these rights a special priority. They protect us, or should, not just from exploitation and overwork, say, but from what is evidently worse – the effects of extreme cruelty or callousness.

'Why are people frequently treated with cruelty or callousness?' is too large a question to enter into here. 'Why are political dissentients frequently so treated?' is scarcely more manageable. We need to distinguish at least two sub-questions: 'Why do those who actually inflict these cruelties do so?' and 'Why do those in power order them to be inflicted or tolerate their infliction?'. So far as the first question is concerned, it seems that always and everywhere, there are cruel and callous men to do these deeds, or else frightened or unprincipled ones who do as they are bid. None of them need share the motives of their masters. The character of their victims as political dissentients is of no relevance to the acts of those who are deliberately cruel or wilfully callous just because they want to be, or just because it is expected of them. These agents of the state would no doubt do the same to any potential victims who fall into their hands. Indeed it has been argued that the state depends upon such agents for its very existence:

> all grandeur, all power and all subordination rests on the executioner: he is the horror and the bond of human association. Remove this incomprehensible agent from the world, and at that very moment, order gives way to chaos, thrones topple, and society disappears.[3]

This deeply conservative conclusion can be understood in a wider sense. And yet we should hesitate before asserting to the picture of licensed brutality that it paints. Those who torture others on behalf of the state have commonly needed training in brutality: it does not come naturally to them.[4] So we should see what they do here as not just licensed, made permissible by the state, but as also made possible by it. The second question, 'Why is it ordered by the state?' has, then, a special priority.

Why are cruelties commonly inflicted on political dissentients by order or permission of the state? One kind of explanation may point to the anger, hatred or contempt which those in power feel for those who refuse assent to their rule. Such emotions may be felt towards enemies without, as much as to the enemy within. When that is so we may expect similar cruelties to be inflicted upon the former. In war those on the enemy side, be they military or civilian, are commonly treated with a degree of cruelty or callousness that serves no military purpose, but rather expresses the hostile attitudes of their opponents. In peacetime it need be no different, for it may be as objects of hostility that political dissentients are treated cruelly, not specifically as citizens registering dissent. As war renders irrelevant our rights to life, liberty and security, so an attitude to certain citizens as to an enemy erodes respect for such rights: cruelty and callousness take over. In this situation we may expect those who give and those who execute orders to inflict cruelties to show a common state of mind. It will rarely be necessary to employ professional sadists when feelings run high against dissentients. Thus those who are in power may attempt to arouse such feelings by feigning them themselves.

A second kind of explanation of cruelty in the treatment of dissentients views it as a purposive rather than an expressive act. Its aim is to intimidate and cow opponents by harsh treatment. Again the same treatment could be meted out to opponents in war with just the same intentions. In each case a calculation is made of the amount of suffering opponents can sustain or risk before capitulating. Whatever the conflict, internal or external, such a calculation can determine policy. And again in neither case does the policy depend upon achieving a perceived violation of rights. Whereas in war, the rights of the enemy, though much attenuated, are specified in international conventions, in peacetime dissenting citizens, as we shall see, have little by way of international protection. A calculation to harm them, then, may be made with little account needing to be taken of adverse consequences. Furthermore the presiding principle which determines the amount of suffering which can rationally be inflicted on an enemy is that of military necessity. While this principle is far from unequivocal, it is operable because the end of war is victory. While one power may wish to inflict such damage on the enemy as to weaken his capacity or his will to fight again, no such secondary purpose is recognised as justifying the infliction of additional suffering. The termination of political dissent is not analogous to military victory. It is a continuing task, not an occasional achievement of governments. In these circumstances there is a temptation to cause excessive suffering with a view to securing the long-term debilitation or demoralisation of an opposition group. Political dissentients are liable, for this reason, to suffer worse treatment than an external enemy. But this can only be so as a result of the contingent facts that an external enemy is more easily able to appeal to international conventions, and is likely to have better protection either from its own resources or from the assistance of others.

GENOCIDE

So far I have tried to argue that the grossness of human rights violation is not to be accounted for by any features special to the political dissentients who are its typical victims. Rather its explanation lies in one or more of the factors that account for cruel or callous treatment of a variety of victims, particularly opponents, external as well as internal, the former lacking the latter's rights. However when it comes to explaining why it is specifically *rights* that are violated the situation changes. The fact that the victims have, or are generally taken to have, certain rights is now essential to the state's ill-treatment of them. The violation of their rights is not simply an accidental feature of the ill-treatment. And now the fact that it is political dissentients who are the victims is in many cases crucial too: for it is the violation of their rights that constitutes the political response to their dissent. It is often specifically as political dissentients – not just as opponents in general – that their rights are violated.

The rights in question are those of personal safety and autonomy which characterise membership of a political community. (Or rather these rights have come to constitute a relation of membership which in former times could not be unequivocally attributed to ordinary folk.) What makes one a member, then, is that the community affords one protection through its laws or customs against assault, pillage or coercion. These rights, have, therefore, a constitutive role, which is presupposed by the secondary rights that attach to people in virtue of their community membership. The violation of these rights by government amounts, therefore, to the withdrawal, suspension or qualification of membership of the political community by its ruling body. Quite independently of any harm that may thereby be done to the victims, the deprivation of membership rights wrongs them in a fundamental way unless they have forfeited their rights for some reason, or unless their apparent rights were previously accorded to them wrongly. Here, although we are concerned with violations, we shall need to examine these defences of deprivation of rights. But first we must look at the kinds of reasons a government might have for deliberately violating what are generally taken to be the constitutive membership rights of some body of people in its territory.

The first case to be considered is that in which a body of people are, or are thought to be, an *obstacle* to state policy. In this case the easiest way for the state to overcome the obstacle may simply be to disregard their rights. In the extreme case this would be to treat them as if they had no community membership rights at all. In the absence of such effective rights – and lacking, of course, the protection of any other political community – they are open to appropriation of property, forced labour or death, as suits the government that violates their rights. Groups of people who encounter such treatment need not be political dissentients, although they are likely to be forced into this stance. They need only be people whose way of life, position in the socio-economic structure or competing interests pose a problem to government that cannot easily be overcome without the violation of their community rights. Aboriginal peoples in the Americas or the Antipodes, certain peasant groups in Stalinist Russia, travelling people in many parts of Europe or the middle classes in Cambodia under the Khmer Rouge, provide examples. The mistreatment of such groups as a means to political objectives is possible because it is thought permissible to disregard their rights for one of two reasons. Either the government takes them not to be, or not fully to be, members of the political community, or it takes their continued membership to be conditional upon changes in their life, or a sacrifice of their interests as a distinctive group, which they are not prepared to make. They are subjected to expropriation, enslavement or genocide as a result of the denial of their community rights.

Genocide encompassed by the internal agencies of the state is the most horrifying example of the violation of rights constitutive of community membership. It is the intended, or foreseeable and preventable, consequence of actions which explicitly or implicitly deny these rights to people who can, by some criterion, be regarded as constituting a distinct ethnic, cultural or socio-economic group. It is, of course, their distinctiveness which makes genocide possible. For the criterion whereby they are regarded as distinct is the converse of that which might qualify them for membership of the political community. It is, for example, white settlers who are viewed as constituting the community, and by that criterion aboriginal peoples form an out-group; or it is the proletariat that constitutes the community, so that landed peasants or urban professionals are excluded.

Genocide is the extinction of a group who cannot be accommodated into a political community so constituted, and for whom no alternative place can be found, either as an under-class in their homeland or as an alien group abroad.

There are, of course, important differences between the examples cited. In some cases there is nothing that a member of the out-group *could* do to qualify himself for community membership. Until the criterion changes the aboriginal remains excluded. By contrast the landed peasant or urban professional can throw in their lot with the proletariat and, in principle, qualify for membership. In these other cases, however, genocide is not a policy to produce compliance by penalising dissent from the political order. Rather it is the treatment meted out to those who are not expected to embrace the political order, and whose compliance might, indeed, be suspect. In both kinds of case, then, the assumption is that the out-group is, entirely or to a high degree, already pre-formed, independently of the will of group members to be, or not to be, part of the political community from which they are excluded.

It is readily apparent that the kinds of state policy to which such groups are likely to form an obstacle are those that depend on identifying the political community with a national group identified by objectively identifiable properties and independently of its members' political will. A group with common ethnic origins provides one example; a group with a common economic interest provides another. Genocide as an intended or foreseeable consequence of mistreatment therefore presupposes this particular view of the political community, which we have labelled the *ethnic* model of nationality. An explanation of genocide is to be sought not only in an account of why a particular group is thought to stand in the way of state policy, but also of why the state should adopt this model of the community. In some cases there will be an overlap here: either the model justifies the ruthless enforcement of policy, or the point of the policy is to make possible the adoption of the model by eliminating counter-examples to a criterion of membership that conforms to it.

It is important to stress how deeply entwined with genocide is the ethnic model of nationality, even if ethnicity can consist in quite different kinds of characterisation. Thus the UN was thinking along the right lines in defining genocide as certain acts 'committed with intent to destroy, in whole or in part, a national, ethnical, racial or religious group, as such' in the 1948 Genocide Convention, and to exclude political groups from its protection.[5] The latter are, in general, possi-

ble targets for a campaign that eradicates opinions and purposes, not
the people who have them. But the distinction is not that easily
drawn. For ostensibly political groups may constitute groups with a
distinctive way of life whether this is thought of in socio-economic or
cultural terms. The Cambodian middle classes subjected to system-
atic genocide by the Khmer Rouge clearly fall into this category,
even though they were identified politically and eradicated for reasons apparently concerned with their political position.

It may be true that genocide is one of a number of options in
nation-state building which includes assimilation or pluralism.[6] But it
is important to see that when it is chosen it recommends itself as part
of the ethnic conception of nationality. Assimilation is compatible
with this conception if ethnicity is thought of in cultural terms: it is
also compatible with voluntarism. But pluralism seems to presuppose
a voluntarist framework. Why did the Khmer Rouge, for instance,
reject these options? Perhaps because defining Cambodian identity
in terms of being a Cambodian peasant eliminated the need to seek
a problematic allegiance as a basis for the legitimacy of a state *both*
communist *and* ethnic nationalist. Whatever the reason,[7] applying
the ethnic model gives the victims of genocide no real choice precisely because it collects others into a state independently of *their*
choices.

It is because the ethnic model is applied to determining national
identity that those who fall outside it, and must in their own interests
oppose it, can be regarded as *enemies*. There is more than an analogy between the way in which the military targets in war are those
who form an obstacle to victory and the way in which the targets of
genocidal policies (or corresponding policies of deportation) are
those who form an obstacle to the success of a certain kind of nation-
state. In these cases what is at issue is its control of territory that is
threatened or hampered by the claims of others upon it or by their
presence (or approach). In both cases, then, those who are obstacles
to control can be thought of similarly as enemies of the state.

There are, of course, two striking but related differences. One is
that in war proper the enemy *intends* to be an obstacle to a certain
state having control of territory, and it uses force to implement its
intentions. An ethnic out-group may simply oppose a certain constitution of the state and use no force at all. The other difference is that
in war it is another state, or a group claiming to act on behalf of or
to inaugurate another or a differently constituted state, that is the

enemy. An ethnic out-group is neither another state nor necessarily politically organised to act in the name of one.[8]

The first difference is overcome by casting the out-group in the role of a *danger* to the state and its proper people, whatever the appearances to the contrary. Thus, under Nazism, the Jews were represented as 'a poisonous parasite ... not only the enemy of our people, but a plague of all peoples'.[9] Some such story is needed if the out-group is to be plausibly thought of as an *enemy* within. But only if it is can the forces of the state be readily mobilised against it in acts of state terrorism or, eventually when the population as a whole swallows the story, in more or less open genocidal war.

The second difference easily disappears from view under the ethnic model. For if the criterion of national identity is some characteristic of people independent of their will, and if, therefore, the state is legitimised by its consisting of people with this characteristic, then those who lack it can be represented in one of two ways. They are foreigners, representatives of some other state, and as such either to be driven back there or killed; or they are antagonistic to the ethnic constitution of states at all, in which case genocide may seem the only final solution. It was as a result of Nazi ideology coming to take the latter view of the Jews as 'cosmopolitan', and hence introducing 'impurity' into all states, that a genocidal policy then seems to have been adopted. But in either case the assimilation of a state and a people, characterised independently of their political associations, makes it possible to intend a war against a people, irrespective of their political organisation.

THE SUPPRESSION OF DISSENT

I said that where a group is an obstacle to state policy the violation of their rights need not constitute a response to *dissent* upon their part, and indeed that the aim of violation may be not to secure their compliance, but to erase their *distinctiveness*. There is an affinity however between dissent and distinctiveness: both can upset a kind of uniformity which is thought essential to the political community. The difference is that distinctiveness upsets a uniformity of objectively discoverable properties; dissent upsets a uniformity of wills. It is with the aim of securing a uniformity of wills that human rights are often violated by governments. But this objective is not to be achieved by treating dissenting wills as an obstacle to be removed. The point of eliminating particular dissentients must then be to prevent others from springing up. In this case violating the rights of dissentients will be an instrument of government, in the proper sense of the phrase.

The suggestion that gross violations of human rights may occur as an instrument of government appears to encounter a major problem. For if the principal purpose of government is precisely the administration of laws which safeguard citizens against attacks that threaten their lives or liberties, how can government itself mount such attacks in violation of the laws or customs of the community? In order to address this latter question we must distinguish a government's overt purpose of administering laws from the less obvious purpose that this presupposes, namely securing the allegiance of citizens to the state. It is, I shall argue, in pursuit of the latter purpose that human rights are commonly violated as an instrument of government.

It is evident that such violations could not normally occur as part of the ordinary enforcement of laws. If the purpose of government is to obtain obedience to the law just because it is the law, then government must also show respect for the law by operating within it. Nor can government legalise acts that constitute violations of human rights without undermining people's faith that the law is to be obeyed because it works to protect them. So government would be unwise to legalise such violations in order to obtain obedience. This is not to say that human rights are never violated in order to enforce the law, nor that human rights violations are never legalised for this purpose. But where they are, I suggest, it is because certain acts which are in fact breaches of law are to be prevented, not because the government wishes to enforce the law as such. For sometimes governments act outside a legal framework to prevent certain acts, for example those which threaten the security of the state, and sometimes they suspend the ordinary operations of the laws for the same purpose. Yet these cases will necessarily be exceptions to the ordinary law-enforcement operations of the state. Where the exceptions are regarded as allowable we do not view it as a violation of human rights. In other cases we consider the government to have overstepped the tightly drawn boundaries of extra-legal action permissible for the prevention of unlawful acts. It is noteworthy that these boundaries are drawn just to permit the government to preserve its *capacity* to govern by ordinary law-enforcement means.

By contrast with this purpose of law enforcement, I suggested, the government aims to secure allegiance to the state. Indeed it must do so if it is to enjoy authority as the body which administers the laws.

People may obey laws because disobedience carries penalties and also because they think the law should be obeyed. Yet they may still not think that the body which exacts penalties is the proper body to do so. And in that case the government rules only by the fact of compulsion or acquiescence, not because its dictates are taken, other things being equal, as prescriptive for conduct. No government can take general obedience for granted in such a situation. Nor can it call on the support of citizens to uphold its claim to administer the law in its territory. Its purpose of law enforcement presupposes, therefore, the securing of allegiance throughout the territory over which it makes this claim.

Allegiance, in this context, is the acknowledgement that a particular state structure in the territory in which one lives is the proper one, so that one owes its government a duty of obedience and support. It is not simply a preparedness to perform one's duty, a preparedness which any government can, on any model of the political community, attempt to enforce by legal sanctions. On the ethnic model it is taken for granted that those who are clear about the objective basis of the political community cannot but acknowledge the propriety of the existing (or aspiring) state. Dissent is simply error or the reaction of an alien group. But evidently such an acknowledgement may be withheld for several reasons, not all of them naturally classifiable in these terms. One may think that the state arrogates to itself powers that properly belong to a different sort of sovereign body (e.g. a monarchy). One may believe that the constitution of the state is undemocratic, so that its government can have no claim on the support of its people. One may hold that the territory in which one lives properly belongs to another state. Or one may feel that a different system of states needs to be created, since the existing state does not reflect national sentiments and thereby lacks legitimacy. In all such cases the withholding of allegiance constitutes political dissent. By *political dissent* is meant here not merely opposition to government policies, but opposition to the state structure within which government policies are made. In order to secure allegiance to the state the government must suppress political dissent. It may well attempt to do so by inducing people to shift their political allegiances.

The notion that it is possible to manipulate allegiance depends on assuming that allegiance lies under the control of the will. That one acknowledges allegiance to a particular state, or would-be state, is not, on this assumption, something that springs naturally and unalterably from one's ethnic, cultural or social situation. The corresponding view of the political community is that of people bound together, not by such common properties, but by a common will. This view, which I have labelled the voluntarist model, is that which provides the ideological basis of the modern Western state. To attempt to secure allegiance by providing inducements to the will therefore presupposes a quite different view of the political community from that presupposed by a policy of eliminating or enfeebling groups which form *obstacles* to the uniform acceptance of rule. In each case one overriding aim of government is the same – to consolidate its power over the people in its territory. But the conception of its relations to those people and its concomitant attitude to them is different. Nevertheless the upshot – the gross violation of the human rights of minorities – may also be deceptively similar in both cases.

Gross violations of human rights frequently occur as a way of pressuring constitutional dissentients to acknowledge allegiance to the existing state structure. It is, I argue, a key part of this strategy not only that penalties attach to dissent which do *in fact* constitute rights violations, but that these penalties *should* constitute violations of membership rights. There are two related reasons for this. In the first place, the allegiance that is sought must be free and uncoerced, and hence cannot be required by law. A political community could not be *constituted* by a common will if that will was the product of coercion. Rather it would be constituted by subordination to the will of the ruling group. If the force of law stems from allegiance to the state that administers it then it cannot be the law that enforces allegiance. It follows that the pressure applied to dissentients cannot be the pressure of the law. Certainly there may be many legal restrictions on the expression or organisation of dissent, imposed for reasons of security, public order or whatever. But in a political community founded on allegiance dissent itself cannot be proscribed by law. The cruelties that constitute gross violations of the human rights of dissentients cannot, therefore, be legitimised as legal penalties for dissent. It follows that they can only be imposed in violation of the dissentients' legal rights. It is as such that these cruelties must appear to citizens – not as legal punishment for dissent, but as its extra-legal consequence, and thus a flagrant violation of their rights.

However, in the second place, since these rights are constitutive of membership of the political community, political dissentients are viewed as forfeiting their rights through refusing to acknowledge allegiance to the state which provides the law-enforcement structure of

the community. Their claim that they are not members of a community so structured is taken at face value, and they are deprived of
the protection that membership affords. On the one hand this is seen
as justifying the violation of their rights. On the other it serves to
demonstrate to them and to others the benefits of membership and
hence to induce both to offer their allegiance to the existing state.
The violation of human rights is hence a comprehensible policy for
a state founded on the principle of allegiance but faced with constitutional dissent which it is unwilling – despite that principle – to
accommodate.

OPPRESSION AND REPRESSION

The situation is, I wish to argue, even worse than this. Gross human-
rights violations are permitted to occur as a response to political
dissent, it seems to me, because we lack answers to two questions.
First, in what circumstances is the suppression of dissent justified?
Second, by what methods is the suppression of dissent permissible?
In the absence of satisfactory answers it is not clear when actions to
suppress dissent can reasonably be undertaken so that unjustified
suppression commonly occurs with a concomitant violation of rights.
Nor is it clear what form political suppression can legitimately take,
so that even violations of human rights are sometimes defended as
necessary to suppress unacceptable levels of dissent.

I cannot, therefore, offer a full answer to the first question: when
is suppression justified? Suffice to say that this will partly depend
upon the effects of the dissent. Certain kinds of expression, organisation and propagation of dissent may, as I indicated earlier, be
suppressed as threats either to public order and safety or to the security and independence of the state. But whereas the first kind of
consideration may seem a purely utilitarian one – many lives may be
saved by inhibiting sectional unrest – the second presupposes the
desirability of the existing state structure. When it is supported by an
overwhelming majority this presupposition may seem reasonable, so
that it may seem justifiable to suppress dissent that threatens the real-
ization of its will. Yet close inspection seldom throws up clear-cut
cases of the applicability of this principle. Sometimes it will not be
clear who the relevant majority is – that in the existing state or that
in a potentially seceding part of it, for example. At other times it will
not be clear that the mere absence of widespread dissent is adequate
evidence of allegiance to the existing state. In any case it is evident

that the mere existence of an assenting majority would not justify suppression of a minority: there would have to be palpable harm or wrong threatening the majority if it was not suppressed. Here – as in the case of weighing the claims of public order against that of freedom to dissent – it is unclear how we are to reach a reasonable judgement.

That said, some cases of suppression of dissent are clearly unjustified and the alleged dangers of dissent are factitious. What stands to suffer is not a majority, but a powerful interest group. We can, for convenience, label cases of the unjustified suppression of political dissent 'oppression'. This catches the notion through alluding to its commonest case – the suppression of dissent (or potential dissent) from one group by a more powerful one in furtherance of its own sectional interests, and thereby contrary to justice. Any oppression will therefore violate the rights of the oppressed group. But these may only be the right to organise and express dissent against the oppressive system. So far it is not only gross violations of human rights that are involved. These, as we have seen, are violations of the rights constitutive of community membership and are, since these rights protect personal security or liberty, cruel or callous acts. Political oppression need not resort to such measures. Freedom of expression and organisation are, other things being equal, human rights. But however flagrantly they are denied in practice this does not constitute what we think of unconfusedly as a gross human-rights violation. Such lesser violations, however, have an inherent tendency towards greater ones. Unjustified suppression tends towards impermissible means.

The reasons for this are twofold. First, oppression breeds a sense of injustice which promotes rather than prevents dissent. Stronger measures are therefore resorted to in a generally fruitless attempt to curb it. Second, the violation of some rights creates a climate of lack of respect for rights in which the limited purposes for which suppression may be justified – public order and security – are lost sight of, and the distinction between attacking manifestations of dissent and attacking the entertaining of dissent itself is blurred. To attempt the latter in the modern Western state must tend, I have argued, to the gross violation of human rights.

The ostensible legality of a great deal of the suppression of political dissent does not, of course, prevent it from being unjustified and hence oppressive. There is, however, a seemingly inexorable slide from ordinary legislative measures, through emergency legislation and martial law, to military suppression which dispenses altogether with the procedures and protections of the law. The slide is induced by the increasing strength and spread of political dissent. On the one hand acts of political violence and on the other mass demonstrations are the usual triggers for extending suppression beyond its ordinary legal limits. In the course of this process dissentients come (in Bentham's words) to be 'looked upon as being no longer members of the State, but as standing altogether upon a footing with external adversaries'.[10] There is, therefore, a concurrence between the view of dissentients presupposed by military action and that which takes them to have forfeited their membership rights by dissenting from the state.

While there are, in wartime, rules determining the treatment of the enemy, and in particular the enemy civilian population, it must be conceded that war puts an end to ordinary expectations of personal security and freedom. We can, therefore, only speak of gross human-rights violations occurring in war when resort to warlike measures is unjustified, or when it is not regulated by the rules of war. The question when *military* suppression of dissent is justified is, again however, one to which there is no accepted answer.

In asking it we are broaching a form of our second general question: what *methods* are permissible in the suppression of dissent? Evidently this must depend on the nature and scope of dissent but certain widely used methods seem clearly impermissible. They constitute, to use a convenient term, 'repression'. I have in mind such acts as opening fire upon demonstrators, placing areas under harsh curfews, removing groups of people from their homes and relocating them away from their means of livelihood, protracted internment and, of course, the torture and killing of individuals. What is wrong with these methods is analogous to what is wrong with acts contrary to the rules of war. As we have seen earlier, broadly speaking only acts that are directed against *obstructions* to military objectives are permissible in wartime. That is why attacks on civilians or ill-treatment of prisoners of war, for instance, are proscribed. The essential objective of military action is to bring under control a piece of territory in which the ordinary law can be enforced, whether as a part of the state or as a zone of occupation. The ultimate objective of suppressing political dissent should be the same. Dissent threatens the state's administration of justice, either directly through creating disorder which cannot be controlled by ordinary law enforcement, or indirectly through endangering national security. To suppress it, therefore, must also be to remove obstructions to the restitution of ordinary law enforcement. Yet the acts of repression which I have instanced go beyond that in various ways. They are acts to deter, demoralise or wreak revenge upon dissentients or upon the group from which they are drawn. They are, for that reason, analogous to acts contrary to the rules of war.

State terrorism can be regarded as lying near the military end of the spectrum of repression. The parallel that I have sketched between repression and war crimes may suggest the common view of state terrorism that I have rejected earlier, which views it, like terrorism in general, as a species of war crime. But though political oppression tends, as it increases, towards war, it is misleading to think of state terrorism in general as a mode of internal warfare waged by the state: it typically lacks the openness of war and partly for this reason denies itself the full resources of a war. Yet while denying itself the resources of war it goes beyond the capacities of ordinary law-enforcement agencies. Its extra-legal aspect is as crucial to state terrorism as its quasi-military one. State terrorism is a crime, in virtue of its being in breach of ordinary legal restrictions, not in virtue of its contravening the rules of war. Its lack of openness renders these rules inapplicable.

For the same sort of reason we cannot expect any framework of rules to bind agents of the state who are engaged in the suppression of dissent, whether by state terrorism or otherwise. The suppression of dissent is not an activity, like war, directed against a hostile group whose presence in a territory wrongs the state by obstructing its administration of justice. Or, rather, this is a view that can be taken only if the dissenting group is regarded as an obstacle to be removed, rather than as opposition to be won over. If the purpose of suppressing dissent, however, is to secure allegiance – as it normally will be in the modern Western state – then the mere existence of a dissentient group cannot be considered to constitute a wrong to the existing state. The group may be justified or unjustified in its claims; it may intend wrong or the upholding of a right; but its dissent cannot constitute a wrong. If it is allegiance that determines the shape of the political community then allegiance cannot be required in such a way that withholding it wrongs a community. It follows that on the voluntarist model the suppression of dissent offers no parallel to the notion of a just cause for war. Without it quasi-military suppression must lack the sincere and open purposes which permit regulation by a system of rules.

Agents of the state usually refuse to concede that they are suppressing dissent in a way analogous to the disabling of enemy forces
so that in both cases a particular, contested, state structure may be
imposed to enforce the law. They will commonly claim instead, that
action is being taken simply to enable law and order to be maintained, and this may be true. For *some* state structure must exist to
enforce the law, and in enforcing the law the particular state structure that does exist is reinforced. What is left out of account is that
political dissentients – with the possible exception of certain anarchists – have no long-term intention to dismantle the law: it is the
structures which enforce it at which they are aimed. Yet in the
absence of some agreed procedures for adjudicating upon their
claims, it is not possible for dissentients to attack the state without
threatening its enforcement of the law. And any state has a duty to
enforce the law. What beyond this the state should do to *maintain* its
hold upon law enforcement is quite unclear.

Here, then, is the nub of the matter. Over a large class of cases the
explanation of the ill-treatment of political dissentients is obscure
because, as I argued earlier, the proper purposes of the state in maintaining itself are unclear. As long as they are unclear, the rights of
dissentients to organise and express dissent will remain undeter-
mined. And while they are, no outline of an acceptable response to
dissent emerges clearly. Then what is evidently unacceptable – the
gross violation of their human rights – continues, since what might
be set in its place stays unspecified.

The *rationality* of gross human-rights violations for which I have
been arguing is, one might say, an amoral rationality. For while we
may condemn certain of such acts as unqualified moral evil, we lack
a sense of the proper political relationships in this area which enables
morality to get a ready purchase. We condemn the evil results, as it
were, of some malfunction in the state, yet we lack a sense of how a
moral mechanism for mediating these relationships might work in
detail. We cannot understand the deviations from the norm that
gross human-rights violations represent when we do not know how
the norm is to be applied in the area of political dissent. At bottom
we lack confidence in how to ground our expectations of reasonable
treatment here.

Chapter 11

The state's response to violence

THE DILEMMA OF THE STATE

Terrorism, I have argued, has the double character of war and crime. Those with a constitutional grievance against the state are often forced into war against it, in the absence of peaceful methods of resolving the dispute. The state has to counter this threat to security if it is to uphold its claim to be responsible for maintaining order within its boundaries. Were the dissentients to constitute an external adversary then it could do so by making a military response. But an internal adversary challenges the state's claim to maintain order. The state typically reacts by appealing to its duty to enforce the law against murder, criminal damage and so forth. It is this, I have claimed, that constitutes the actions of the state's adversary as *terrorist*. The terrorist knowingly confronts the state with a dilemma: either to be treated as a military threat, risking the state's claim to maintain order by enforcing the law, or to be treated as a criminal, risking the state's security. Either way it will look as if the state is failing in one of its duties to its citizens: what should it do?

If the constitutive purpose of the state is to enforce the law, and if state terrorism and similar forms of state action against political dissentients are illegitimate because they are in breach of the law (or at least of just law), then it might seem to follow that the state's proper recourse against political violence is to enforce the ordinary law against it; that is to say, to apprehend, put on trial and punish the perpetrators for crimes of murder, wounding, criminal damage and so on. And this is, perhaps, the state's usual recourse, at any rate in Western democracies.

The explanation of this is clear. Since in a democratic state there is held to be a comprehensive method for settling grievances, any resort to violence is considered to be unnecessary. Thus there is no reason not to regard it as simply criminal. What is more, to do anything else would apparently concede part of the terrorist's case, namely that the state is not simply using its power to enforce the law; it is using it to prevent constitutional change. But this will raise a question the state would prefer to remain closed, the question of its own legitimacy. Treating violent opposition as criminal provides no opportunity to open the question, while it expresses the state's assumption of its legitimacy as the proper power to enforce the law against any who are a threat to order.

Two points need to be made. First, as we have seen, it is just not true that democratic procedures permit the peaceful resolution of all disputes, particularly in the case of disagreements over nationality. The state would not in fact be making any concessions in its claim to legitimacy by declining to treat its opponents in such cases as breaking rules of political conduct, precisely because in these cases there are no rules which they are breaking. One reason for treating their actions as *simply* criminal disappears.

Second, although it seems tempting to suppose that the state must express a claim to legitimacy by treating terrorists as criminals this overlooks the fact that such a claim may equally be expressed by military measures. The state's use of military force to preserve security against internal adversaries no more represents a concession of its claim to legitimate rule than the use of military force against external aggressors. All that can be said is that treating terrorists as criminals may persuade people that the state is legitimate, since to treat them as criminals implies that they have an obligation to obey its law, which would not automatically accrue to an illegitimate state. But this is a matter of tactical expediency, not of the political or ethical duty of the state.

Indeed the modern state's disinclination to treat terrorists as anything but criminals reflects its interest in being regarded as an association for the maintenance of the order and security essential to social life. So viewing it, citizens are brought to identify themselves with the state as that on which their settled life depends. Their natural desire for social stability is translated directly into loyalty to the existing state. For if a state is such an association, then it is prudent to treat a violent challenge to it as a crime, for otherwise it appears to risk the breakdown of social life – the Hobbesian 'warre of every man against every man' – which its ostensible purpose is to prevent.

What is in the interests of the state, however, may not be what benefits the citizens it serves.

The state, even when it claims legitimacy, has no *obligation* to punish terrorist action as criminal. As we noticed in discussing the normative model of law, acts directed against the state can be distinguished from crimes against the community. Of course terrorist acts result in death and suffering to ordinary members of the community as well as to agents of the state. But from the fact that the state is constituted through its role of safeguarding the rights of community members by law enforcement, it does not follow that in every case the appropriate way to protect them is by law enforcement. If acts which threaten community members are principally directed against the state then it may be that they should be treated differently from ordinary acts of violence. The state's duty of protection to the community may be discharged, for example, as in an external war of defence.

On the positivist model of law it is natural to suppose that any requirement to treat terrorism as ordinary crime would derive from the overall benefits it brings, by contrast with those of other policies. We are dealing with judgements of relative utility here, but judgements, it should be said, relativised to the society the state claims to represent, and thus not ones that terrorists – for example those espousing secessionist causes – would necessarily accept. Does the violence with which the state is concerned, however, always favour criminalisation? It is not clear that it does.

Suppose, as Bentham maintains, that

> the business of government is to promote the happiness of the society, by punishing and rewarding. The part of its business which consists in punishing, is more particularly the subject of penal law. In proportion as an act tends to disturb that happiness, in proportion as the tendency of it is pernicious will be the demand it creates for punishment.[1]

Then the utilitarian point of the penal law is to regulate the behaviour of members of society for its common good. While the penal law may be effective against isolated criminals it is not clear that it works against terrorists. So Bentham recognises that there are

> pernicious enterprises . . . backed with a greater quantity of physical force than the persons who are in a more particular sense officers of justice are wont to have at their command . . . accord-

ingly, when the persons by whom it is perpetrated are in such force as to bid defiance to the ordinary efforts of justice, they loosen themselves from their original denomination in proportion as they increase in force, till at length they are looked upon as being no longer members of the state, but as standing altogether upon a footing with external adversaries.[2]

Mischief from these is to be dealt with not by police action but by military force. Bentham provides us then with one possible utilitarian argument for excluding terrorists, or rebels as he would term them, from the ambit of the ordinary criminal law.

This, however, is to distinguish different cases of terrorism and to use utilitarian criteria for choosing which tactics to adopt. The utilitarian need not accept that if legal remedies are ever appropriate then in legally similar cases they should always be. But he must accept that if the state decides that utilitarian considerations sometimes render them inappropriate, then equally, in applying them, it is treating law enforcement as a particular tactic. While this tactic may have a utilitarian justification in serving the public interest, it does not derive any moral advantage from its being a legal process that is applied. Indeed the utilitarian justification for using the law may be to give an *appearance* of mere criminality to a pernicious military threat that might otherwise win adherence.

The dangers of this pragmatic approach are evident. If the state can pick and choose which tactic to adopt it risks blurring the distinction between war and police action. This not only gives the consequent appearance of doing injustice to the state's opponents, who may be denied the rights either of combatants or of criminals: it also runs the risk of state terrorism, in which covert military action accompanies overt law enforcement. Some have wanted to pursue this pragmatic middle way. Thus while Sidgwick maintains that 'it is admitted by all reasonable persons that it is the imperative duty of every government to punish wrongful violence directed against itself like other wrongful violence – and even with peculiar severity on account of the widespread evils resulting from anarchy,'[3] he also argues that those captured in a widespread insurrection should be accorded prisoner of war status. Besides prudential reasons Sidgwick offers a moral one: 'the mere strength and extent of an insurrection must be taken to show that a large number of persons regard it as justifiable'.[4] That terrorists do not recognise the legitimacy of the state is held to exonerate them, at least partially, of crimes against it. It is hard to see, however, how such sharply contrasting modes of treatment as criminal punishments of 'peculiar severity' and prisoner of war status can be morally justified simply on account of the degree of public support for a campaign of political violence.

The doctrine of international law is that prisoner of war status is not applicable to a state's own citizens. Rather 'subjects taken in arms against their lawful prince are not considered as prisoners of war, but as rebels: and are liable to the punishments ordinarily inflicted on rebels', as was stated in the trial of the rebel Scots in 1745.[5] It is hard however to find any moral justification for this principle, which seems simply to benefit those who uphold a certain state structure, rather than the community at large. That said, rebels fall into a *distinct* category from ordinary criminals precisely because their actions are directed against the state rather than the community.[6] To treat them differently from ordinary criminals – even if by way of punishments 'of peculiar severity' – is to acknowledge this important difference. For it is one thing to treat terrorists as criminals – all it requires is that there be laws which are enforced against them – it is another thing to treat them as *ordinary* criminals or *simply* as criminals. For ordinary criminals are punished for failing to respect the rights of members of the community, not for failing to respect the state. To punish someone for the latter is consistent with not treating him simply as a criminal. It is consistent, for example, with the granting of amnesties and pardons, admission to negotiations and so forth, for reasons quite unconnected with any reconsideration of the offences punished. That the state should adopt such tactics rather than continue to treat the offences as crimes is intelligible and often justifiable. But to the extent that the state thinks of its choices in this way it is no longer regarding its violent opponents as *terrorists*: to do that it must treat them *simply* as criminals. This is not, I have argued, forced upon the state. Indeed the political and moral justification for it is, I shall suggest, open to question. Paradoxically, however, the state's insistence that terrorists are mere criminals is frequently accompanied by measures that differentiate them from ordinary criminals. Denied political status in prisons they are nonetheless tried in special courts, subjected to prolonged investigative detention or given peculiarly severe sentences. And these are justified by the special dangers terrorists pose, as if those were the dangers of particularly ruthless and well-organised crooks, when evidently they are the dangers of unresolved political issues.

MILITARY RESPONSES

One alternative to a law-enforcement strategy against violent political opponents is the employment of military force. In some circumstances its use may become inevitable in an irresolvable conflict between an intransigent state and a strong opponent. But should it not be a response of a last resort? Could an attitude to those currently treated as terrorists that they are simply waging a war better conduce to the good of citizens in circumstances where law enforcement remains a viable option?

The conventional wisdom is that it could not. 'Far from promoting people's good' it may be contended that 'this is a recipe for the collapse of liberal democracy itself, and for the murder squads and anarchy that, in other countries, breed misery, fear and oppression'.[7] War is indeed a terrible evil. But it is not necessarily the greatest of all evils and, while it is not my intention to prescribe behaviour for the state, it needs to be recognised that in refraining from a military stance the state may be serving interests other than those of the community it claims to represent.

A military response offers advantages to the state's opponents as well as additional dangers; and this may be why a strong state, confident or careless of its legitimacy, will not be lured into it. In particular it is the response that terrorists seek – at least overtly. If they have an arguable grievance which cannot be resolved politically it may be the most *just* way of treating them, for it treats them as moral equals of the state. At first sight this may seem a hollow concession. The state is likely to be, after all, not an equal militarily, but a superior. Justice, therefore, may well not prevail. This is not the point. Nothing will ensure that a just cause prevails in war. Applying the norms of war, however, permits one's adversary to be treated in a way that allows for the possible justice of his cause. It is compatible with the continuation of the political process in a way that treating him as a mere criminal is not.

My first point, then, is that justice may sometimes lie on the side of responding to violent opposition as to war. This is, I think, readily conceded in those situations where the state has lost confidence in the justice of its own cause – where it continues to act as a colonial power, for instance. Then, faced with the prospect of war, it may accede to negotiations in which it has to question its own claims. It is this result that an insistence that the state treat a terrorist challenge as war, rather than as crime, is partly intended to achieve. But it is an insistence which represents a particular political stance, unavailable where the state has no tendency to question its own legitimacy. Citizens, however, had better beware of such an attitude. The good that they seek to secure is that which comes from members of communities living a better life together than they do while unresolved conflicts continue among them, erupting into sporadic violence. There is, of course, no guarantee that the outcome of war or of the threat of war will secure this. Their outcome is determined by many factors besides strength of communal feeling and the consequent conviction of having a just cause. But it is determined in part by this, which cannot easily be set aside if the good life of the state's citizens is to be achieved.

To persistently treat political opponents as criminals is to blur the distinction between the law-enforcement function of the state, performed for the good of citizens, and its maintenance of power, which may or may not be pursued for the good of citizens. Citizens need to be able to distinguish these activities clearly if they are to make an accurate judgement of whether the present state structure is in their interests or not. The state would do well to avoid an attitude to its adversaries which militates against this and to adopt one of respect for their competing claim to power. Such an attitude is at least possible in war (though it must be admitted that the traditions of chivalry which facilitate it are increasingly under threat from the moral certainties of powerful states).

The second kind of argument one might mount for a military response to terrorism is that it may actually on balance cause less harm to citizens than law-enforcement methods. Two scenarios are possible here. One is that of a crushing blow designed to eliminate the terrorist threat; the other of essentially defensive operations on a continuing basis. The first is likely to be misguided. An internal adversary cannot be driven back to his own borders like an external aggressor. He either gives up or he is disabled militarily. In the former case he lives to fight another day. In the latter he is either liquidated or more or less permanently imprisoned. In these latter cases methods of political suppression will have to be resorted to that go beyond what is justified by resort to war. It is these possibilities of which those who oppose the military option are rightly apprehensive.

But it is less clear that a defensive war attracts the same criticism. Indeed the main point of using military methods will be to provide better protection for ordinary citizens. If a state of war is openly acknowledged then the rules of war which are principally designed to protect civilians could be applied – and insisted upon – by both sides. In the same spirit precautions could be taken to prevent civilians from becoming the victims of attack, which cannot be taken in the ostensible normality implied by law-enforcement methods. Admittedly the recent history of warfare should not lead one to be too sanguine, but nor has the record of the state in preventing harm to their citizens by criminalising terrorism been a spectacular success.

It is not perhaps too cynical to suggest that the protection of citizens from terrorist attack in the short term is not often the primary objective of the state. The occurrence of attacks which kill and maim harmless women and children can be a valuable propaganda weapon against the terrorist cause. If terrorists could succeed in restricting their victims to the agents of the state it would be unavailable. But the state would only be assisting in this by mounting an effective military defence. It would also, of course, be publicly displaying the limitations of its own law-enforcement capacity. The state can usually avoid this by taking it upon itself to determine at what point, in terms of harm to its citizens, these capacities have run out. In doing this the state's interest in retaining power may take precedence over its purpose of protecting its citizens through law enforcement.

There are other more easily demonstrated ways in which the immediate protection of citizens is not always the primary aim of law enforcement policies. First, the *apprehension* of terrorists demands an appearance of normality which would be disturbed if civilians were given the protection afforded by a military presence. Second, when open war is not countenanced covert military operations frequently take place. But for them to remain covert, civilians are exposed to risks over and above those involved in ordinary guerrilla warfare. They are, for example, caught in the crossfire following 'stake outs', which are of necessity unpublicised. Furthermore, to avert attention from the political effectiveness of terrorists in disrupting ordinary life, warnings of bombs are not always acted upon speedily and comprehensively in a way that best protects civilian life. In sum, the assumption that terrorists must be pursued and brought to justice rather than contained and rendered as harmless as possible can, in the short term at least, imperil ordinary civilians.

Comparisons here are distasteful and will take us well beyond the scope of the philosopher's legitimate interest. My observations are intended to dispel any assumption that an *a priori* verdict can be returned against a military option. Such an assumption stems, it would appear, from a Hobbesian apprehension that relaxing the operation of domestic law unleashes the 'warre of every man against every man' that knows no rules or constraints. Talk of a war against terrorists as 'a recipe . . . for murder squads and anarchy'[8] strongly suggests the influence of this assumption. But wars do have rules and murder squads are contrary to them. Indeed death squads are principally employed not in open war, but where the state's challengers are ostensibly regarded as criminals yet cannot be suppressed by the ordinary forces of law and order. In short, they are instruments of state terrorism rather than of warfare proper.

Acts of state terrorism would be contrary to the rules of war were they to occur in wartime: death squads as often liquidate the civilian supporters of revolution as they kill armed revolutionaries. It is such acts, on both sides, which the acknowledgement that a state of war exists should tend to prevent. Were they not prevented they could, even in wartime, be treated as crimes. For acts in wartime that involve the murder of civilians and so forth remain crimes against ordinary domestic law and may be tried as such, as well as counting as war crimes or crimes against humanity punishable by international tribunals.

It may be objected that this is seldom feasible. International terrorism in particular provides many examples of atrocities against civilians whose states have no way of bringing those responsible to justice. In these and other cases, e.g. in occupied territories, retaliatory strikes are commonly resorted to. But difficult as the position of such states is, retaliatory strikes often lack a properly *military* purpose. Were they to take place in open war many would count as reprisals proscribed by the rules of war, because they target civilians.[9] They have no justification as a tactic of countering international terrorism any more than they would as a counter to internal terrorism where, it is apparent, they would be employed only by ruthlessly repressive regimes. Once again departures from properly military methods cannot be used as an argument against the use of properly military methods for countering terrorist threats.

CONCILIATION

A policy of criminalisation makes it hard for the state to negotiate with its armed opponents, or at least to negotiate publicly. Just as it is inappropriate to do deals with bandits, since the rule of law is thereby prejudiced, so, it is often supposed, it is inappropriate to negotiate with terrorists. This line of argument fails if, as I hope to have shown, the state has no obligation to treat terrorists as mere criminals. Furthermore, without negotiations the terrorists' grievances are unlikely to be addressed and violence continues. The question arises whether there are good grounds for refusing to negotiate with terrorists in order to attempt to resolve the issues that lead to violence.[10]

Two kinds of argument are commonly mooted against negotiation and, more widely, against the political recognition of terrorists that it implies. The first I shall deal with only briefly, since philosophical considerations seem of limited application to it. It is that negotiation with terrorists strengthens their hand and therefore weakens the effect of security measures taken against them, whether these be of a law-enforcement or military character. The argument against negotiating over a political settlement will claim, for example, that it will gain further active support for terrorists against whom it is difficult to act effectively for fear of prejudicing the negotiations. The force of the argument, as of many similar arguments in this area, is hard to assess. But the very fact that it is hard to assess should make us wary. The long-term consequences of our actions are in general incalculable. With the best intentions in the world we can do enormous harm. Yet unless we have very strong reasons for suspecting that the harm we cause will outweigh the intended benefits, we are right to continue in our course. The alternative is moral cynicism or despair. In the kind of case under discussion, acting out of the suspicion that initiatives for peace have adverse consequences overall often reflects pessimism or a lack of moral commitment. An honest attempt to achieve a political settlement is compatible with a due concern for immediate security.

A quite different type of negotiation – too often confused by politicians with those that aim at a political settlement – concerns such questions as truces, the release of prisoners and the like. The principal argument offered against such negotiations from considerations of security is that concessions to terrorists encourage them in the kinds of action that provide bargaining counters – notably the taking of hostages. The situations involved vary. Where on the one side terrorists are held as criminals and on the other agents of the state are taken prisoner, my earlier arguments would permit exchange in accordance with the ordinary usages of war. Whether this is prudent is a matter for judgement in particular cases. The notion that released terrorists have been wrongly granted immunity does not have force if their criminal prosecution and imprisonment is itself simply a tactic of the state. On the other hand, where civilian hostages are taken, contrary to the rules of war, and are to be exchanged for those who are clearly war criminals the situation is different. Perhaps all that can usefully be said is that no compromise on general principles of justice is involved when action is taken *in extremis* from humanitarian motives, and in this case the certainty of immediate benefits may outweigh the uncertain chance of long-term drawbacks. Evil is seldom the monopoly of one side in a conflict, and it is beyond doubt that a policy of criminalising terrorism serves the turn of many states by retaining a pool of those who are in effect themselves hostages for potential exchange.

A second and philosophically more interesting argument against negotiations with terrorists is that it concedes to them a legitimacy that they have forfeited through resort to violence. The argument can be filled out in different ways. One again rests its case on the claim that terrorism is merely criminal. But since, I have argued, it is the state's attitude which makes it criminal, not the intentions of the terrorist, this can scarcely be a good reason for the state to refuse to enter negotiations. A second filling out of the argument broadly maintains that any resort to violence is in breach of the conventions of debate required for negotiations. The men of violence are barred from them, much as a philosopher was, as I once heard, barred from seminars for punching his fellow symposiasts. But while an *argumentum ad baculum*[11] is indeed contrary to the conventions of philosophical debate, because its appearance changes the nature of that debate, the menace of possible coercion is part of the common currency of political negotiation. Terrorists are little different from other participants in what they threaten.

A third more plausible development of the argument claims that political debate in a *democracy* depends upon a shared understanding that the contending parties will leave it to the people to decide the issue. Support for terrorism betokens a disinclination to accept this understanding, and therefore disqualifies its supporters from playing a part in the political process. Part of my reply to this argument is by now predictable. It is that the debate which terrorists seek to enter is seldom one on which the people – in their ordinary political role as voters choosing between contenders for office within an established state – are able to adjudicate. Most terrorist campaigns are waged in

support of constitutional changes to established states – most signifi-
cantly those that would involve changes to state boundaries and
hence to the electorate. It is the absence of democratic means for
resolving such disputes that principally explains the emergence of
terrorist campaigns. It follows directly that terrorists cannot in these
cases be regarded as adopting illegitimate methods through rejecting
the understanding which underlies democratic decision making.

The remaining element in a reply to this argument accepts that
democratic processes in a broad sense *are* relevant to resolving the
dispute. The democratic argument depends on interpreting the
notion that we should leave something for the people to decide as
leaving it to be decided on the basis of their preferences. This in its
turn implies, the argument runs, leaving it to be decided on the basis
of what they want, by contrast with what they are constrained to
choose under threat of violence. However, the implied contrast
between desire and coercion drawn by analogy from cases where
people literally have a gun pointed at their heads is far-fetched.
Violence may affect the political issue, but seldom by constraining
people to choose one option in quite this way.

Sometimes, no doubt, violence will also affect people's judgement
by inducing fear: they might be intimidated into supporting the solution that would not commend itself to them if they were free of the
fear of violence. However, were people *not* to be fearful they would
fail fully to grasp a point highly relevant to the decision they are
called upon to make: namely the strength of the terrorist's indignation and the contraction of his human sympathies. Likewise they will
need to know the resolve and ruthlessness of those who control
power in the existing state. It is an inescapable fact that those with
grievances will sometimes turn to violence and that the state will use
force against them. To exclude those who employ coercive tactics
from negotiations is simply to exclude a whole class of cases from
being decided by, in the broad sense, democratic processes. That
these often operate under coercive pressures is unavoidable.

The contrary view may sometimes reflect the voluntarist doctrine
often conflated with the principle of democracy, namely that the constitutional structures of states should reflect people's desires to
associate freely. On this doctrine citizens have a right not just to
decide between contenders for power within the existing state but to
determine what structures there should be. The emphasis on *free*
association marks a contrast with associations forced upon people,
and which they accept only for fear of adverse consequences. Thus

in seeking to negotiate on constitutional changes those who threaten violence are allegedly unprepared for the outcome to reflect free association in which everybody's preferences count equally.

Not only is this a deeply unrealistic picture of any actual negotiating situation, the theoretical difficulties of implementing it in a plebiscite have already been noted. If, however, it is a picture that the terrorist accepts then he must justify his resort to violence as the result of being blocked in his desire for a plebiscite of a kind satisfactory to himself – one covering the whole of Ireland, say, in the case of IRA demands. So long as there is no obvious available way of translating popular wishes into changed state structures uncontentiously, there is no good argument that terrorism aimed at changing them is not a legitimate political position. On the other hand, if the terrorist rejects the voluntarist picture in favour of an ethnic model of nationality, for instance, he will not be impressed by its presuppositions as to how an eventual decision on his claim should be made. In neither case, then, is there a good argument for regarding his resort to violence as rendering him not a legitimate party to negotiation.

The foregoing discussion brings into prominence to what extent whether someone is admitted as a legitimate partner in political discussion or not is a matter of which rules the state chooses to apply. This is most obviously the case in the exclusion of 'mere criminals' which reflects the state's attitude that turns its opponents into 'terrorists'. As ordinary criminals their threat constitutes *intimidation* – the *private* act of individuals conspiring to use force against their fellow citizens: it is not viewed as a political and therefore a *public* act – the warning of the use of force to achieve political objectives. The proscription of terrorist organisations as merely criminal conspiracies serves to exclude them from the permitted sphere of public speech and action within which any negotiations must take place. But this way of defining that space is a politically, not a philosophically, motivated one.[12]

There may be ideological reasons for a state to regard some groups as legitimate participants in negotiations and to bar others. Sometimes this will have to do with the grounds the state offers for its own legitimacy claims. Thus an ethnically grounded state can only view the pursuit of different aspirations to statehood, contrary to the existing structure, as rebellion, whether by full citizens or by members of an ethnic minority. In the first case rebels may be regarded as actors in a public political drama, though there is no point in admitting them to negotiations, since their disagreement is one of *fact*, not of a divergence of wills which might be resolved by mutual compromise. They are not legitimate participants because they deny the article of belief on which any political debate between citizens of that state depends. In the second case they are simply not full members of the state entitled to enter such a debate.

The voluntarist model which underpins most modern Western nations' legitimacy cannot regard those who have desires to associate differently from those of the majority within the state as thereby disbarred from political participation. It may, as we have seen, proscribe them if they use violence to attempt to change the basis on which that majority is constructed. But since, if the state shows no willingness to reconsider this basis, they may have no alternative to violence for changing it, their proscription again reflects a political choice by the state. Their lack of legitimacy is the result of this choice.

HUMAN RIGHTS

What is the *point* of negotiating with internal terrorists if part of their reason for violence is that they are radically at odds with the assumptions on the basis of which the state might conduct negotiations? What, for example, might be achieved by a democratic state founded on voluntarist principles negotiating with religious fanatics[13] or with racists? This question is the large and difficult one of whether those who make radically different assumptions about the nature of nations or states can settle the disputes that arise as a result by rational debate. It is the question of whether there can be a framework for political debate on constitutional questions that does not itself close off some possibilities.

One somewhat pessimistic conclusion is that there cannot: only against a background of a system of liberal states, it is said, is such a framework possible. That makes negotiation with those who reject liberal assumptions – e.g. various kinds of ethnic nationalists or Marxist revolutionaries – impossible, if the aim is to accommodate something of what each party is seeking in an eventual state structure. By liberalism here I shall understand the view that each citizen should be free to pursue his or her own conception of the good life, subject only to each accepting constraints which prevent undue restrictions on the freedom of others.[14] What is debatable within liberalism is how precisely this condition is to be spelt out, but that is not our concern here. Two points about liberalism are important. One is that it offers no conception of a *social* good – a good life for society – other than the successful pursuit of what the members conceive to be good. Second, liberalism implies a voluntarist framework for social organisation since part of each citizen's conception of the good life is a view about who to associate with. It follows, on my understanding of the terms, that liberalism is incompatible with communitarian conceptions of society, including Marxist or religious ones, and with ethnic conceptions of the nation.

Yet, it may be observed, liberalism has overwhelming advantages because it guarantees human rights of life, liberty and equal consideration as the conditions needed for each person to pursue their conception of the good. To compromise on liberal principles in order to buy peace with those who dispute them must, it may be claimed, put the human rights of citizens in jeopardy. This argument is unsound. Only if liberal principles provided the *sole* basis for human rights would this conclusion follow. But, I shall suggest, there are other more fundamental reasons for respecting them. What is more, they are precisely the sort of reasons that generate an explanation of how it is possible to enter political debate with people who espouse radically different principles.

Whatever their differences as to how people should be grouped in ways that generate a right to statehood (or analogous forms of political organisation) and whatever their differences as to what statehood (or political organisation generally) should be, those who hold views on such issues will agree on one thing: that the political organisation to be sought is the one that is best for the group of people seeking it or on whose behalf it is being sought. Those who seek *private* benefits rather than some putative *public* good cannot be regarded as holding views about *political* organisation, as it is understood in the modern world by contrast with the organisation of private property or servants and the dispensing of patronage.[15] Yet those who seek what is best for their group by way of political organisation cannot deny its members rights of life, liberty and equality of treatment, since these are just the rights necessary to membership of any politically organised community: they are what political organisation protects. Nothing would count as such a community without them, not because of their indispensability to individual projects, but because it is essential to any communal project – including the liberal one – that it is carried out in accordance with respect for such rights.

Why, though, should governments concede these rights to those they do not regard as properly entitled to membership of the community? The reason surely is that any *actual* political community falls well short of any ideal one. But to the extent that it satisfies the conditions of a community by respecting human rights it is a better place. Indeed one kind of objection to the status quo on the part of oppressed minorities is precisely that these conditions are not fulfilled, and this is a complaint that can and is made by people with very different views of what the community should be like. Other things being equal, everyone has an interest in the actual community being no worse than it need be. Yet other things are seldom equal in the situation of constitutional debate which is currently under consideration. For here at least one party is assumed to want changes in the actual community, and to contemplate a possible temporary worsening of it through violence in order to produce something closer to their ideal. One kind of case does indeed lie beyond the reach of any rational resolution, and that is where one party can see no scope for degrees of improvement short of the complete attainment of their ideal. Millenarians of this stamp have no interest in the good of the existing political community: their only interest lies in its supercession. But such a position is rare, confined perhaps to religious enthusiasts and to genocidal racists, neither of whom would normally wish to enter ordinary political debate. It certainly comprises a much smaller class than those who dispute the principles of liberalism.

The majority of political actors can envisage degrees of improvement or deterioration in the actual political community as it approximates more or less to their ideal scenario. It is as fellow participants in their actual community that they are able to negotiate with others with a view to effecting what both can see as an improvement. This creates a possible common good despite very different conceptions of the social good or very different views of how the boundaries of communities should be drawn. It also sustains an interest in preserving human rights so long as scope exists for improvement by negotiation.

The picture I am describing is one in which both parties seek to accommodate their disparate ideals to the structures currently existing. Attenuated and evanescent though the bonds which these structures create may be, they nonetheless presuppose the possibility of some common projects, including the preservation of human rights. But no one can engage in a common project with others without having or finding some common ground for discussion of how to achieve it, alongside other projects they have as individuals or members of other groups. It may not be apparent to the participants what common ground they share, and yet share it they do, and, sharing it, are able to discuss better ways in which their projects can be realised. Yet this is only to say that they can negotiate on ways in which political structures can be improved from both their points of view.[16]

What I am stressing here, as in my earlier discussions of the common-good model of nationality, is the discrepancy between what *is* the case, so far as people's principles are concerned, and what they *take* to be the case. This does not imply that actual political communities are *really* all right just as they are. Certainly they may not be. Most obviously, as I mentioned a moment ago, some will scarcely be communities at all, so slender is the protection of human rights which they afford. Less obviously, where human rights are respected the pursuit of a *common* good thereby, even if this is conceived as an aggregate of individual goods, may play little part in social life. This does not require, but is sometimes assisted by, a common conception of what is worthwhile in a society and a commitment to it by its members. It is for this reason that groups with different conceptions are often capable of living better common lives when they form their own political communities. Yet this is not necessarily so, in particular where conception and reality come badly apart.

Failure to appreciate the existence of common ground within functioning – even if badly functioning – political communities stems from a dangerous intellectualism which looks for principles in pronouncements rather than in deeds. It is this, in consequence, which leads to a disinclination to negotiate when explicit principles are radically opposed. In particular, demands are made for the acceptance of liberal principles as a condition for entry to negotiation. The motives for such demands in terms of the protection of human rights are laudable. But it is, I have suggested, simply doctrinaire to suppose that liberal principles are the only safeguard here, or the only foundation for rational political debate. Such doctrinaire attitudes go no way towards encouraging debate. Indeed they foment political violence which risks violating and denying the very rights they ostensibly defend.

Notes

1 INTRODUCTION

1 For an account which places the notion of a political community within the general framework of human relationships see Gilbert 1991, ch. 7.

2 TERRORISM AND UNJUST WAR

1 E.g. Lorenz 1966: for criticism of such sociobiological theories see Kitcher 1985.
2 Freud 1961, p. 111.
3 Teichman 1986, p. 96. See also Teichman 1989; Wallace 1993.
4 Cf. Clark 1988, pp. 31–2.
5 Cf. LaCroix 1988, p. 141.
6 Anscombe 1981, p. 53. For related discussion, see Nagel 1979, pp. 53–74.
7 See Paskins and Dockrill 1979, p. 221–36.
8 Vitoria (1480–1546) quoted in Bailey 1972, p. 12.
9 It is, I suggest, confusion as to whether punitive or defensive theory is being applied that often leads to mutual incomprehension between terrorists and the public concerning the former's choice of targets.
10 Cf. Domingo de Soto (1495–1560), reported in Bailey 1972, p. 13; and Phillips 1984, p. 33.
11 Cf. Paskins and Dockrill 1979, p. 225.
12 Cf. Walzer 1977, pp. 25–7.
13 As is argued by George 1990, 1992.
14 See Wallace 1989, and for criticism of the terrorist's use of such arguments Wallace 1991.
15 E.g. Suarez (1548–1617), quoted in Bailey 1972, p. 10.
16 See Bailey 1972, p. 88.
17 Teichman 1986, p. 97.
18 Chamberlain's description of area bombing as 'mere terrorism' (quoted in Coady 1985, p. 57) gains its rhetorical point precisely by its hyperbolic departure from ordinary usage.

19 Cf. Hughes 1982, p. 5.
20 See Fotion and Elfstrom 1986, pp. 220–4.

3 TERRORISM AND CIVIL WAR

 1 E.g. George 1988.
 2 Cf. Coady 1985, p. 65 who defines terrorism as a type of 'revolutionary violence'.
 3 An aspect of the Marxist use of just war notions: see Clark 1988, pp. 46–7.
 4 See Gilbert 1987 in reply to Simpson 1986 for an example.
 5 Cf. Teichman 1986, pp. 40–5.
 6 E.g. George 1992.
 7 E.g. Phillips 1990.
 8 E.g. Walzer 1977, pp. 195–6.
 9 Ibid.
10 See LaCroix 1988, pp. 67–9, 142–3.
11 Quoted in Clark 1988, p. 89.
12 See Bailey 1972, pp. 64–5.
13 LaCroix 1988, p. 256.
14 Jenkins 1961, ch.1.
15 *Pace* Walzer 1977, p. 185.
16 Cf. Hughes 1982, p. 5 who defines terrorism as 'a war in which a secret army – one whose members have other occupations, wear no uniforms and do not otherwise admit their membership openly – spreads fear'. My way of characterising irregulars allows that they may comply with the Geneva Conventions by having a 'fixed distinctive sign' and by carrying their arms openly: see Bailey 1972, p. 83.
17 Cf. Benn 1988, pp. 189–98 for an account of these effects of coercive terror.
18 E.g. Phillips 1984, pp. 89–93.
19 Ibid. p. 93 (cf. Clark 1988, p. 95).
20 Ibid. p. 94 (cf. Walzer 1977, p. 187).
21 See Walzer 1977, pp. 147–59.
22 E.g. Phillips 1984, p. 98.
23 Ibid. p. 89.
24 Hobbes 1914 (1651), pt. 1 ch. 13.
25 Mabbott 1947, pp. 21–2.

4 TERRORISM AND POLITICAL CRIME

 1 Following LaCroix 1988, ch. 7.
 2 See Walzer 1977, pp. 86–108.
 3 See Walker 1984, p. 224; Ramose 1992, p. 13.
 4 Third Geneva Convention (1977) Protocol 1 Articles 1–4. See LaCroix 1988, p. 267; Walker 1984, pp. 217–19; O'Brien 1991, p. 93.
 5 See Bailey 1972, pp. 85–6.

6 See Walker 1984, pp. 191–2, 201.
7 Cf. Sidgwick 1891, p. 238.
8 See Lodge 1981a, p. 170.
9 Lodge 1981b, p. 5.
10 Ibid. p. 1.
11 Walzer 1977, pp. 199–200.
12 Cf. Gosling 1990, p. 86.
13 Some writers take coercion to involve limiting the choices of others abnormally (e.g. Nozick 1972, p. 116), or limiting them unfairly (e.g. Haksar 1986, p. 50). For further discussion see Wertheimer 1988.
14 See Lomasky 1991.
15 But not all, *pace* Murphy 1975, p. 1.
16 E.g. Raphael 1976, p. 46.
17 Mair 1962, pp. 45–7.
18 Clausewitz 1987 (1832) pt. 1, ch. 1, s. 24.

5 COMMUNITY AND CONFLICT

1 For a general discussion of communitarianism see Kymlicka 1990, ch. 6.
2 Vitoria, quoted in Bailey 1972, p. 12.
3 Hobbes 1914 (1651) ch. 13. For discussion see H. Williams 1992, ch. 6; Airaksinen and Bertman 1989.
4 E.g. Wilkins 1992, pt. 1, pp. 19–32 and pt. 2.
5 Cf. Cooper 1972.
6 For a discussion of whether collective responsibility is reducible to individual responsibility see Cooper 1968; Wilkins 1992, pt. 2.
7 See Beran 1987.
8 By contrast with a *community*, as understood in the contrast between *Gesellschaft* and *Gemeinschaft* due to Tönnies 1971, pp. 131–7.
9 Cf. LaCroix 1988, pp. 172–3.
10 E.g. Honderich 1989, ch. 3.
11 E.g. Phillips 1990; cf. O'Sullivan 1986a.
12 See George 1992, who regards this as a crucial aspect of terrorist ideology.
13 See Gilbert 1991, ch. 6, s. 3.

6 REASONS FOR VIOLENCE

1 E.g. Honderich 1989, ch. 6.
2 See Billington 1980, p. 356; Linse 1982.
3 E.g. Lomasky 1991.
4 See above, ch. 4, 'Political crime'.
5 Ibid.
6 Rawls 1973, s. 55.
7 Frazier 1972, p. 324.
8 *Pace* Rawls 1973.

9 The Gandhian approach: see Haksar 1986, chs 1–2; cf. Parekh 1986.
10 For a discussion of Marxist violence see Parekh 1992.
11 For a discussion of 'the leader principle' see O'Sullivan 1983, pp. 149–59.
12 Quoted in Habermas 1974, p. 82.
13 For a recent account see Taylor 1982.
14 Corresponding to the two forms of political address noted above, 'Alternatives to violence'.

7 TERRORISM AND NATIONALITY

1 Wilkinson 1977, p. 40.
2 See G. Graham 1992.
3 Barker 1947, p. 274.
4 Ivor Jennings, quoted in French and Gutman 1974, p. 138.
5 Corresponding roughly to the 'substantive' and 'procedural models' for a right to secede introduced by Buchanan 1991, pp. 132–5.
6 E.g. Beran 1987, pp. 37–42.
7 Sidgwick 1891, pp. 621–2.
8 See Beran 1987, pp. 34–6.
9 Quoted in Benn 1967, p. 443.
10 A *realist* model would make the existence of a nation *independent* of anyone's ability to discover that it existed; see Vision 1988, ch. 1.
11 That is, not just *causally* voluntarist, so that willings *constitute* a nation and do not merely *produce* one; see below, 'State and community'.
12 Cf. Mill 1861b, ch. 4. It is worth remarking that desiring something does not produce the conditions of satisfaction. Thus a shared desire for statehood does not procure the conditions necessary for it – a suitable scale, geographical cohesion and social stability. See below, ch. 8 'Culture and power'.
13 Mill 1861a, ch. 16.
14 See above, ch.5, n. 8.
15 Hobbes 1914 (1651), chs.17–18.
16 As held by Locke, in Barker 1947, pp. 80–1.
17 See Wilson 1988.
18 See Buchanan 1991, pp. 38–45.
19 Mill 1861a, ch. 16.

8 ETHNICITY AND NATIONAL IDENTITY

1 D. Miller 1989, p. 244; see also D. Miller 1993.
2 Kohn 1946, p. 9.
3 Hamilton Fyfe, in Snyder 1964, p. 68.
4 This contrast relates to, but is not identical with that between 'Continental' and 'Whig' theories of the nation due to Kedourie 1960, pp. 131–3, and that between 'ethnicist' and 'statist' accounts proposed by Smith 1983, ch. 7 and his 'ethnic' and 'civic' models 1991, ch. 1.

5 See Billington 1980, pp. 57–71.
6 Cf. Mabbott 1947, p. 164: 'one seems driven back on the view that any group of people who feel they are a nation are a nation. Yet if nothing but a belief unifies the group the belief must be an illusion'.
7 Quoted in Kedourie 1960, p. 106.
8 Mazzini 1907, p. 52.
9 Herder, in Zimmern 1939, p. 165.
10 Firth 1938, p. 16.
11 The celebrated distinction between 'le droit du sang', and 'le droit du sol' currently under threat in France.
12 E.g. Ardrey 1967: see above, ch. 2. 'Mindless violence' for further discussion.
13 Cf. Shaw and Wong 1989.
14 Mazzini 1907, p. 52.
15 In Snyder 1964, p. 90.
16 In Zimmern 1939, p. 169.
17 Locke 1961 (1690a), bk. 2. ch. 27.
18 The similar notion of 'collective memory' due to Halbwachs is discussed by Burke 1989, pp. 97–113.
19 Court of Appeal judgement that Rastafarians do not form such a group: *Guardian* law report 1.2.93.
20 As noted by Bishop Butler, in Perry 1975, p. 45.
21 Or at least requires it: cf. B.A.O. Williams 1973.
22 Mazzini 1907, p. 55.
23 Ibid., p. 52.
24 See MacCana 1985.
25 And it is hard to agree that a 'right to self-determination derives from the value of membership in encompassing [i.e. ethnic] groups' just because for many such groups the value of membership is questionable, *pace* Margalit and Raz 1990.
26 Quoted in Smith 1991, p. 26.
27 I owe the idea of this account to suggestions by David Miller.
28 Sidgwick 1891, p. 217.
29 Beran 1987, p. 42.
30 Locke, in Barker 1947, pp. 80–1.

9 TERROR AND THE STATE

1 Wilkinson 1977, p. 152.
2 Cf. Honderich 1989, pp. 191–202.
3 E.g. Mrs Thatcher's Guildhall speech, 14.11.88.
4 Cf. Paskins and Dockrill 1979, p. 89.
5 See Merkl 1982 and Noakes 1986.
6 Nor can state terrorism plausibly be seen as motivated by attempts at the 'maintenance of order', *pace* Stohl 1979, p. 9. Vigilantes, in or out of uniform, are not as such terrorists, though terrorists may act as vigilantes. For vigilantes, by their own lights, mete out justice, however

rough. State terrorism is not very rough justice, for it is control, not legal or quasi-legal order, that it seeks to impose.

7 *Pace* Coady 1985, p. 65.
8 See Honderich 1989, ch. 4.
9 See Cohen 1974.
10 See Petersen 1982, p. 278.
11 Cf. McCoubrey 1987, p. 139.
12 Sidgwick 1891, p. 162.
13 Mill 1859, fn.1.
14 The distinction is due to Rawls 1955 and used by Milne 1986, pp. 14–15.
15 Quoted in McCoubrey 1987, p. 134.
16 Giddens 1985, p. 19.
17 Raphael 1976, p. 46.
18 Although it would beg fewer questions about the identity of nations to call it state security.
19 Reported as Blackstone's view in G. Williams 1957, pp. 112–13.
20 For a discussion of the motives for criminalisation see Walker 1984.

10 THE VIOLENCE OF THE STATE

1 Articles 3 and 5.
2 Ibid. article 24.
3 De Maistre, quoted in Ryan 1991, p. 240.
4 See Glover 1991, pp. 268–9.
5 See Freeman 1991b, p. 4.
6 Freeman 1991a, p. 21.
7 See Hawkesworth 1988, ch. 6 for discussion of various theories.
8 A more complicated formulation is required than one that contrasts between states with war on people, as supposed by Lemkin: see Freeman 1991b, p. 4.
9 Quoted in Lackey 1991, p. 154 fn. 6.
10 Bentham 1789, fn. 228.

11 THE STATE'S RESPONSE TO VIOLENCE

1 Bentham 1789, ch. 7, s.1.
2 Ibid., fn. 228.
3 Sidgwick 1891, pp. 263–4.
4 Ibid.
5 Quoted in Walker 1984, pp. 212–13.
6 See above, ch. 4. 'Terrorism as crime', ch. 9 'The force of law'.
7 W.W. Miller 1989, p. 57.
8 Ibid.
9 See Bailey 1972, p. 53.
10 See Schmid 1988 and Hughes 1988.
11 See Hamblin 1970, pp. 44, 156–7.

12 Similar considerations apply to, e.g., the British Broadcasting Ban on
   terrorists, see Gilbert 1992.
13 See Sprigge 1992.
14 Cf. Nino 1991, pp. 92–101.
15 Though no doubt there are still many who do not 'enter into Parliament
   with such exalted hopes', but 'in the service of one's friends', as Gibbon
   remarked in 1760, quoted in Namier 1957, p. 18.
16 See K. Graham 1986, ch. 6.

References

Airaksinen T. and Bertman M.A. (eds) (1989), *Hobbes: War among Nations*, Aldershot: Avebury.

Almond B. and Hill D. (eds) (1991) *Applied Philosophy: Morals and Metaphysics in Contemporary Debate*, London: Routledge.

Anscombe G.E.M. (1981) *Collected Philosophical Papers*, Vol. III, Oxford: Blackwell.

Ardrey R. (1967) *The Territorial Imperative*, London: Collins.

Bailey S.D. (1972) *Prohibitions and Restraints in War*, London: Oxford University Press.

Barker E. (ed.) (1947) *Social Contract: Essays by Locke, Hume and Rousseau*, London: Oxford University Press.

Benn S. (1967) 'Nationalism' in P. Edwards (ed.) *Encyclopedia of Philosophy*, NY: Macmillan.

Benn S. (1988) *A Theory of Freedom*, Cambridge: Cambridge University Press.

Bentham J. (1789) *An Introduction to the Principles of Morals and Legislation* (reprinted 1961 *The Utilitarians*, New York: Doubleday).

Beran H. (1987) *The Consent Theory of Political Organisation*, London: Croom Helm.

Billington J.H. (1980) *Fire in the Minds of Men: Origins of the Revolutionary Faith*, London: Temple Smith.

Buchanan A. (1991) *Secession*, Boulder, CA: Westview.

Burke P. (1989) 'History as Social Memory' in T. Butler 1989 (ed.) *Memory: History, Culture and the Mind*, Oxford: Blackwell.

Clark I. (1988) *Waging War: A Philosophical Introduction*, Oxford: Oxford University Press.

Clausewitz, K. von (1987) [1832] *On War* (trans. M. Howard and P. Paret) Princeton, NJ: Princeton University Press.

Coady C.A.J. (1985) 'The Morality of Terrorism', *Philosophy* 60.

Cohen M. (1974) 'Morality and the Laws of War', in V. Held, S. Morgenbesser and T. Nagel (eds) *Philosophy, Morality and International Affairs*, Oxford: Oxford University Press.

Cooper D. (1968) 'Collective Responsibility', *Philosophy* 43.

Cooper D. (1972) 'Responsibility and the 'System', in P. French (ed.)

Individual and Collective Responsibility, Cambridge, MA: Schenkman Publishing Co.

Firth R. (1938) *Human Types*, London: Nelson.

Fotion N. and Elfstrom G. (1986) *Military Ethics: Guidelines for Peace and War*, London: Routledge.

Frazier C. (1972) 'Between Obedience and Revolution', *Philosophy and Public Affairs* 1.

Freeman M. (1991a) 'Genocide and the Political Community', *Essex Papers in Politics and Government* 84.

Freeman M. (1991b) 'Speaking about the Unspeakable: Genocide and Philosophy', *Journal of Applied Philosophy* 8.

French S. and Gutman A. (1974) 'The Principle of National Self-determination', in V. Held, S. Morgenbesser and T. Nagel (eds) *Philosophy, Morality and International Affairs*, Oxford: Oxford University Press.

Freud S. (1961) *Collected Psychological Works* Vol. XXI, London: Hogarth Press.

George D. (1988) 'Distinguishing Classical Tyrannicide from Modern Terrorism', *Review of Politics* 50.

George D. (1990) 'Terrorists or Freedom Fighters', in M. Warner and R. Crisp (eds) *Terrorism, Protest and Power*, Aldershot: Edward Elgar.

George D. (1992) 'Armed and Unarmed Struggle: Ideology in Terrorism', in B. Almond (ed.) *Terrorism in the New Europe*, Hull: SVRC.

Giddens A. (1985) *The Nation State and Violence*, Cambridge: Polity.

Gilbert P. (1987) 'Just War: Theory and Application', *Journal of Applied Philosophy* 4.

Gilbert P. (1989) 'Terrorism: War or Crime?', *Cogito* 3.

Gilbert P. (1990a) 'Community and Civil Strife', in M. Warner and R. Crisp (eds) *Terrorism, Protest and Power*, Aldershot: Edward Elgar.

Gilbert P. (1990b) 'Terrorism: The Right Response?', *Cogito* 4.

Gilbert P. (1991) *Human Relationships: A Philosophical Introduction*, Oxford: Blackwell.

Gilbert P. (1992) 'The Oxygen of Publicity: Terrorism and Reporting Restrictions', in A. Belsey and R. Chadwick (eds) *Ethical Issues in Journalism and the Media*, London: Routledge.

Gilbert P. (1993) 'Criteria of Nationality and the Ethics of Self-determination', *History of European Ideas* 16.

Glover J. (1991) 'State Terrorism', in R.G. Frey and C.W. Morris (eds) *Violence, Terrorism and Justice*, Cambridge: Cambridge University Press.

Gosling D. (1990) 'Rawls in the Non-ideal World: an Evaluation of the Rawlsian Account of Civil Disobedience,' in M. Warner and R. Crisp (eds) *Terrorism, Protest and Power*, Aldershot: Edward Elgar.

Graham G. (1992) 'Liberalism and Democracy', *Journal of Applied Philosophy* 9.

Graham K. (1986) *The Battle of Democracy: Conflict, Consensus and the Individual*, Brighton: Wheatsheaf.

Habermas J. (1974) *Theory and Practice*, London: Heinemann.

Haksar V. (1986) *Civil Disobedience, Threats and Offers: Gandhi and Rawls*, Delhi: Oxford University Press.

Hamblin C.L. (1970) *Fallacies*, London: Methuen.

Hawkesworth M.E. (1988) *Theoretical Issues in Policy Analysis*, Albany, NY: State University of New York Press.

Hobbes T. (1914) [1651] *Leviathan*, London: Dent.

Honderich T. (1989) *Violence for Equality: Inquiries in Political Philosophy* (third edition) London: Routledge.

Hughes M. (1982) 'Terrorism and National Security', *Philosophy* 57.

Hughes M. (1988) 'Terror and Negotiation', unpublished manuscript.

Jenkins R. (1961) *The Dilessi Murders*, London: Longmans.

Kedourie E. (1960) *Nationalism*, London: Hutchinson.

Kitcher P. (1985) *Vaulting Ambition: Sociobiology and the Quest for Human Nature*, Cambridge, MA: MIT Press.

Kohn H. (1946) *The Idea of Nationalism: A Study in its Origins and Backgrounds*, NY: Macmillan.

Kymlicka W. (1990) *Contemporary Political Philosophy: An Introduction*, Oxford: Oxford University Press.

Lackey D.P. (1991) 'Extraordinary Evil or Common Malevolence: Evaluating the Jewish Holocaust', in B. Almond and D. Hill (eds) *Applied Philosophy: Morals and Metaphysics in Contemporary Debate*, London: Routledge.

LaCroix W.C. (1988) *War and International Ethics: Tradition and Today*, Lanham, MD: University Press of America.

Linse H. (1982) "Propaganda by Deed" and "Direct Action": Two Concepts of Anarchist Violence', in W.J. Mommsen and G. Hirschfeld (eds) *Social Protest, Violence and Terror in Nineteenth and Twentieth Century Europe*, London: Macmillan.

Locke J. (1961) [1690a] *An Essay Concerning Human Understanding*, London: Dent.

Locke J. (1947) [1690b] *Second Treatise on Civil Government*, in E. Barker (ed.) *Social Contract: Essays by Locke, Hume and Rousseau*, London: Oxford University Press.

Lodge J. (1981a) 'The European Community and Terrorism: Establishing the Principle of "Extradite or Try"' in Lodge 1981b.

Lodge J. (ed.) (1981b) *Terrorism: A Challenge to the State*, Oxford: Robertson.

Lomasky L.E. (1991) 'The Political Significance of Terrorism', in R.G. Frey and C.W. Morris (eds) *Violence, Terrorism and Justice*, Cambridge: Cambridge University Press.

Lorenz K. (1966) *On Aggression*, New York: Harcourt Brace.

MacCana P. (1985) 'Early Irish Ideology and the Concept of Unity', in R. Kearney (ed.) *The Irish Mind: Exploring Intellectual Traditions*, Dublin: Wolfhound.

McCoubrey H. (1987) *The Development of Naturalistic Legal Theory*, London: Croom Helm.

Mabbott J.D. (1947) *The State and the Citizen: An Introduction to Political Philosophy*, London: Hutchinson.

Mair L. (1962) *Primitive Government*, Harmondsworth: Penguin.

Margalit A. and Raz J. (1990) 'National Self-determination', *Journal of Philosophy* 87.

Mazzini J. (1907) *The Duties of Man and Other Essays*, London: Dent.

Merkl P.H. (1982) 'Approaches to Political Violence: the Stormtroopers

1925–33', in W.J. Mommsen and G. Hirschfeld (eds) *Social Protest, Violence and Terror in Nineteenth and Twentieth Century Europe*, London: Macmillan.

Mill J.S. (1859) *On Liberty*, reprinted in Mill 1910.

Mill J.S. (1861a) *Representative Government*, reprinted in Mill 1910.

Mill J.S. (1861b) *Utilitarianism*, reprinted in Mill 1910.

Mill J.S. (1910) *Utilitarianism, Liberty, Representative Government*, London: Dent.

Miller D. (1989) *Market, State and Community*, Oxford: Oxford University Press.

Miller D. (1993) 'In Defence of Nationality', *Journal of Applied Philosophy* 10.

Miller W.W. (1989) 'Terrorism: A Reply', *Cogito* 3.

Milne A.J.M. (1986) *Human Rights and Human Diversity*, London: Macmillan.

Murphy, J.G. (ed.) (1975) *Civil Disobedience and Violence*, Belmont, CA: Wadsworth.

Nagel T. (1979) *Mortal Questions*, Cambridge: Cambridge University Press.

Namier L.B. (1957) *The Structure of Politics at the Accession of George III*, London: Macmillan.

Nino C.S. (1991) *The Ethics of Human Rights*, Oxford: Oxford University Press.

Noakes J. (1986) 'The Origins, Structure and Functions of Nazi Terror', in N. O'Sullivan (ed.) *Terrorism, Ideology and Revolution*, Brighton: Wheatsheaf.

Nozick R. (1972) 'Coercion', in P. Laslett, W.G. Runciman and Q. Skinner (eds) *Philosophy, Politics and Society* (fourth series), Oxford: Blackwell.

O'Brien W.V. (1991) *Law and Morality in Israel's War with the PLO*, New York: Routledge.

O'Sullivan N. (1983) *Fascism*, London: Dent.

O'Sullivan N. (1986a) 'Terrorism, Ideology and Democracy', in O'Sullivan 1986b.

O'Sullivan N. (ed,) (1986b) *Terrorism, Ideology and Revolution*, Brighton: Wheatsheaf.

Parekh B. (1986) 'Gandhi's Theory of Non-Violence: His Reply to the Terrorists', in N. O'Sullivan (ed.) *Terrorism, Ideology and Revolution*, Brighton: Wheatsheaf.

Parekh B. (1992) 'Marxism and the Problem of Violence', *Development and Change* 23.

Paskins B. and Dockrill M. (1979) *The Ethics of War*, London: Duckworth.

Perry J. (ed.) (1975) *Personal Identity*, Berkeley, CA: University of California Press.

Petersen J. (1982) 'Violence in Italian Fascism 1919–25', in W.J. Mommsen and G. Hirschfeld (eds) *Social Protest, Violence and Terror in Nineteenth and Twentieth Century Europe*, London: Macmillan.

Phillips R. (1984) *War and Justice*, Norman, OK: University of Oklahoma Press.

Phillips R. (1990) 'Terrorism: Historical Roots and Moral Justifications', in M. Warner and R. Crisp (eds) *Terrorism, Protest and Power*, Aldershot: Edward Elgar.

Ramose M.B. (1992) 'Wars of National Liberation and the Laws of Armed Conflict', in A.G.D. Bradney (ed.) *International Law and Armed Conflict*, Stuttgart: Steiner.

Raphael D.D. (1976) *Problems of Political Philosophy* (second edition), London: Macmillan.

Rawls J. (1955) 'Two Concepts of Rules', *Philosophical Review* 64.

Rawls J. (1973) *A Theory of Justice*, Oxford: Oxford University Press.

Ryan A. (1991) 'State and Private: Red and White', in R.G. Frey and C.W. Morris (eds) *Violence, Terrorism and Justice*, Cambridge: Cambridge University Press.

Schmid A.P. (1988) 'Force or Conciliation?', *Violence, Aggression and Terrorism* 2.

Shaw R.P. and Wong Y. (1989) *Genetic Seeds of Warfare: Evolution, Nationalism and Patriotism*, London: Unwin Hyman.

Sidgwick H. (1891) *The Elements of Politics*, London: Macmillan.

Simpson, P. (1986) 'Just War Theory and the IRA', *Journal of Applied Philosophy* 3.

Smith A.D. (1983) *Theories of Nationalism*, London: Duckworth.

Smith A.D. (1991) *National Identity*, Harmondsworth: Penguin.

Synder L.L. (ed.) (1964) *The Dynamics of Nationalism*, Princeton, NJ: Van Nostrand.

Sprigge T.L.S. (1992) 'Fundamentalism and International Law', in A.G.D. Bradney (ed.) *International Law and Armed Conflict*, Stuttgart: Steiner.

Stohl M. (ed.) (1979) *The Politics of Terrorism*, New York: Dekker.

Taylor M. (1982) *Community, Anarchy and Liberty*, Cambridge: Cambridge University Press.

Teichman J. (1986) *Pacifism and the Just War*, Oxford: Blackwell.

Teichman J. (1989) 'How to Define Terrorism', *Philosophy* 64.

Tönnies F. (1971) *On Sociology: Pure, Applied and Empirical*, Chicago: Chicago University Press.

Vision G. (1988) *Modern Anti-Realism and Manufactured Truth*, London: Routledge.

Walker C.P. (1984) 'Irish Republican Prisoners – Political Detainees, Prisoners of War or Common Criminals?', *The Irish Jurist* 19.

Wallace G. (1989) 'Area Bombing, Terrorism and the Death of Innocents' *Journal of Applied Philosophy* 6.

Wallace G. (1991) 'Terrorism and Argument from Analogy', *International Journal of Moral and Social Studies* 6.

Wallace G. (1993) 'The Language of Terrorism', *International Journal of Moral and Social Studies* 8.

Walzer M. (1977) *Just and Unjust Wars*, New York: Basic.

Wertheimer A. (1988) *Coercion*, Princeton, NJ: Princeton University Press.

Wilkins B.T. (1992) *Terrorism and Collective Responsibility*, London: Routledge.

Wilkinson P. (1977) *Terrorism and the Liberal State*, London: Macmillan.

Williams B.A.O. (1973) 'Are Persons Bodies?', in his *Problems of the Self*, Cambridge: Cambridge University Press.

Williams G. (1957) *Salmon on Jurisprudence*, London: Sweet and Maxwell.

Williams H. (1992) *International Relations in Political Theory*, Milton Keynes: Open University Press.

Wilson H.A. (1988) *International Law and the Use of Force by National Liberation Movements*, Oxford: Oxford University Press.

Zimmern A. (ed.) (1939) *Modern Political Doctrines*, London: Oxford University Press.

Index

Hitler, Adolf 17
Hobbes, Thomas 38–42, 62–4,
   100, 138, 160, 167
human rights 133, 142–4, 146–7,
   150–8, 172–5

India 112
individualism 74, 76
innocents 11–16, 50, 60, 62, 74–5,
   80
insurgency 29, 31–3, 39, 46, 52,
   55, 59
involuntarism 109
IRA 4, 13, 23, 25, 47–8, 51, 171
Ireland 23, 25, 38, 48, 94–5, 112,
   130, 171
Israel 19
Islam 91–2
Italy 133

Jews 150
jihad 83
jus ad bellum 8–10, 21, 28–9, 55
jus in bello 8–10, 11, 55
just war, theory of 7–20, 21–5, 45,
   57–8, 59–60; defensive version
   8–10, 13–20, 23; punitive
   version 8–10, 11–13, 14, 22, 24,
   53

Khmer Rouge 147, 149
Klefts 30

liberalism 93, 172–5
Locke, John 115–16

Mafia 30
Marxism 71, 72, 75, 87, 128,
   172–3
Mazzini, Giuseppe 110, 113,
   117–18
memory 115–16
Mexico 32
Mill, John Stuart 99, 134
modernity 71–6

national identity 3, 93–105,
   106–25, 148–50, 160, 175

nationalism 72, 75, 108, 109–25,
   149, 172
Nazism 130, 133, 135, 150
negotiation 161–72, 175
normativism 138–9, 161
Nuer 56

oppression 155–6
Ottoman Empire 30

Pakistan 112
patriotism 33
Peru 22
positivism 45–7, 57, 59, 133–40,
   161

racism 110–12, 116–17, 174
RAF 43
realism 100, 109–10, 124
Red Brigades 43
Renan, Ernest 98
repression 156–8
revolution 22–8, 30, 33, 51, 64, 66,
   70–1, 77, 84–92, 95, 102, 108,
   130, 131, 167, 172; liberal 85,
   87–8, 91, 102; national 102;
   socialist 87–9
Rousseau, Jean-Jacques 29, 94
Russia 77, 111, 147
Russian Revolution 87

secession 41–2, 46, 52, 55, 65, 94,
   105, 120–1, 161
security 3, 10, 40, 55–6, 58, 128,
   136–7, 141, 151, 156, 159, 168
self-defence 8–10, 13–20, 25, 67
self-determination 46, 72–4,
   96–105, 122–3
self-government 101–3
Sendero Luminoso 22
Sidgwick, Henry 96, 122, 134, 162
sociobiology 112
Somalia 41
South Africa 46
sovereignty 24, 57, 58, 72–4
Soviet Union 95, 111
Stalinism 147
state, the 12, 20, 26, 31, 35, 39–40,
   45–7, 50, 52, 54–8, 61, 62–76,